Teaching

MONEY
APPLICATIONS
to Make # MATHEMATICS
MEANINGFUL

Grades 7–12

Teaching

MONEY
APPLICATIONS
to Make MATHEMATICS
MEANINGFUL
Grades 7–12

**Elizabeth
MARQUEZ**

**Paul
WESTBROOK**

*Foreword by
Charlotte Danielson*

CORWIN PRESS
A SAGE Publications Company
Thousand Oaks, CA 91320

For information:

Corwin Press
A Sage Publications Company
2455 Teller Road
Thousand Oaks, California 91320
www.corwinpress.com

Sage Publications Ltd.
1 Oliver's Yard
55 City Road
London EC1Y 1SP
United Kingdom

Sage Publications India Pvt. Ltd.
B 1/I 1 Mohan Cooperative
 Industrial Area
Mathura Road, New Delhi 110 044
India

Sage Publications Asia-Pacific Pte. Ltd.
33 Pekin Street #02-01
Far East Square
Singapore 048763

Printed in the United States of America

Library of Congress Cataloging-in-Publication Data

Marquez, Elizabeth.
Teaching money applications to make mathematics meaningful, grades 7–12 / Marquez, Elizabeth, Westbrook, Paul.
   p.cm.
Includes index.
ISBN-13: 978-1-4129-4138-9 (cloth)
ISBN-13: 978-1-4129-4139-6 (pbk.)
   1. Mathematics—Study and teaching (Middle school)—United States. 2. Mathematics—Study and teaching (Secondary)—United States. 3. Money—United States. I. Westbrook, Paul. II. Title.
QA11.2.M2675 2007
510.71'2—dc22

                                                      2006101120

This book is printed on acid-free paper.

07   08   09   10   11   10   9   8   7   6   5   4   3   2   1

Acquisitions Editors:	Jean Ward and Hudson Perigo
Editorial Assistants:	Jordan Barbakow and Cassandra Harris
Production Editor:	Melanie Birdsall
Typesetter:	C&M Digitals (P) Ltd.
Copy Editor:	Gillian Dickens
Proofreader:	Cheryl Rivard
Cover Designer:	Lisa Riley

Contents

Foreword

Research has solidly established the importance of teaching mathematics in authentic contexts because they engage student interest. Research has also revealed that high school seniors are deficient in knowledge of personal finance basics, such as investments and credit card debt.

Here are some discouraging items:

- People younger than age 25 are the fastest-growing group filing for bankruptcy.
- Six of out 10 high school students get a failing grade on economics.
- The personal savings rate was −0.5% in 2006, the first time since 1933.

People of note have weighed in on this subject:

- Federal Reserve chairman Ben Bernanke said that financial literacy for both the young and old is a topic of vital importance to the nation's economic future.
- Argus Research economist Richard Yamorone said that given the ever-expanding decisions people face, it is especially crucial that they sharpen their financial skills: "It's not a subject that anyone can afford to fail."

Money is a topic that engages students and that frequently requires mathematical knowledge in order to be understood. By infusing finance into required, standards-based math classes, *Teaching Money Applications to Make Mathematics Meaningful, Grades 7–12* gives students the opportunity to learn the mathematics that is addressed in every set of state standards while simultaneously learning the basics of finance essential to every successful life.

Elizabeth Marquez, master math teacher, and Paul Westbrook, accomplished financial planner, have written a book that is a valuable resource in the quest for mathematical and financial literacy. *Teaching Money Applications to Make Mathematics Meaningful, Grades 7–12* offers practical ways to use money concepts to teach mathematical concepts as it first guides teachers through basic financial territory, to the extent that they need it, and then offers a handbook on how to teach mathematics in financial contexts. Teachers of prealgebra through calculus and statistics will find rich teaching examples throughout the book that they can use instead of the less engaging and less important examples they may have been using.

Teaching Money Applications to Make Mathematics Meaningful, Grades 7–12 is an important book for all who care about students' acquisition of both mathematical literacy and financial security. It provides guidance for teachers in how to engage students with important mathematical concepts in the context of real-life applications. Moreover, it provides a response to that demanding student question, "When am I ever going to have to use this stuff?" In answering that question, this book can help all students appreciate the beauty and applicability of mathematics while preparing for a healthy financial life.

—Charlotte Danielson
Educational Consultant

Introduction

Math and money, perfect together! Why? Teachers know that student engagement is key to achievement, and they know that when money is the topic, there is genuine interest and improved performance. As many teachers have witnessed, students who have trouble with basic computations seem to have no trouble when money is involved. This book makes the most of that engagement and improved performance by using money to interest students in mathematics that goes beyond basic computation. It engages student interest in topics that appear in every set of state mathematics standards. At the same time, this book builds financial literacy that is desperately needed since the average high school graduate lacks the basic money skills critical to success in life.

Chapters are offered on a wide range of money topics within which standards-based mathematics can be presented and reinforced. Among other things, teachers are shown how they can use annuities to teach geometric series, stock market trends to teach measures of central tendency, credit card debt to teach exponential functions, risk to teach standard deviation, supply and demand to teach geometric transformations, and the cost of owning a car to teach regression. Exposure to these topics will, at the very least, make students aware of money matters that affect their lives and the mathematics that help them understand those matters.

Each chapter is structured in the following way:

- First, National Council of Teachers of Mathematics (NCTM) content and process standards covered in the chapter are listed. In this, a wide range of math topics is addressed, depending on the chapter, from pattern recognition, present/future value, statistics, graphs, and tables to use of graphing calculators and computer spreadsheets, among others. You will note a particular emphasis on present/future value because this is basic to understanding the role that money plays in our lives.
- Second, valuable background information on money subjects is given. This will allow a teacher a chance to review the subject being covered.
- Third, and the heart of the book, are the teaching examples provided, starting with basic skills, processes, and concepts and moving to more complicated mathematics. Projects and extensions are also suggested.

To further help the teacher, we have provided a comprehensive glossary of money terms, a math locator, a comprehensive index, and a summary of formulas.

Between the authors, we have many years dedicated to teaching mathematics and to financial planning. We hope this book will help you help your students to become mathematically and financially literate.

Please contact us if you would like to share your teaching experiences with this subject or if you think there are ways this book can be improved. You can reach us through our e-mail: authors@mathteachers.com.

PUBLISHER'S ACKNOWLEDGMENTS

Corwin Press gratefully acknowledges the contributions of the following reviewers:

Joyce Deer, NBCT
Math Teacher
North Pike High School and
    Middle School Virtual School
Summit, MS

Lyneille Meza
Math Teacher
Strickland Middle School
Denton, TX

Kathleen Choma
Math Teacher
South Brunswick High School
Monmouth Junction, NJ

Mary Kollmeyer
Math Teacher
Lejeune High School
Camp Lejeune, NC

Edward C. Nolan
Mathematics Department
    Chairperson
Albert Einstein High School
Kensington, MD

Mark Yates
Secondary Mathematics and
    Physics Teacher
Northfield Mount Hermon School
Northfield, MA

Debra A. Scarpelli
Math Teacher, PAEMST 2003
Pawtucket, RI

Math Locator

By Chapter and Teaching Examples Within Chapters

Math Topic	Chapter							
	1	2	3	4	5	6	7	8
	Teaching Example							
NUMBER AND OPERATIONS	1, 2, 3	1, 2, 3	1, 2	1, 2, 3, 4	1, 2, 3	1, 2, 3	1, 2	1, 2
Computation	1, 2, 3	1, 2, 3	1, 2	1, 2, 3, 4	1, 2, 3	1, 2, 3	1, 2	1, 2
Percent Increase/Decrease				1, 2	2	2		
Percents	1, 3	1, 2, 3	1	1, 2	1, 2	1	2	1, 2
Proportions/Ratios	2	1		1	1			
ALGEBRA	1, 2	1, 2, 3	2	3, 4	1, 2, 3	3	1	2
Distributive Law		2						
e		2		3		3		
Explicit Formulas	1, 2	1, 2, 3	2		1, 2, 3			
Exponential Equations		2, 3	2		1, 2, 3			
Exponentiation		2, 3			1, 2, 3	3		
Functional Notation					3			
Linear Equations				4	3		1	2
Logarithms		2						
Pattern Generalization	1	1, 2, 3	2					
Recursive Formulas			2					
Sequences		2						

(Continued)

(Continued)

Math Topic	Chapter							
	1	2	3	4	5	6	7	8
	Teaching Example							
Series		3						
Sum of Functions					3			
System of Equations					3		1	2
Tables of Values	1	2, 3	2		2		1	2
GEOMETRY				2, 3	3	1, 3	1	2
Graph Interpretation				2, 3	3	1, 3	1	2
Plane Transformations							1	
DATA ANALYSIS	2		2	1, 2, 3, 4		3		
Correlation Coefficient	2			4				
Data Representation: Table, Charts, Graphs	2			1, 2, 3, 4		3		
Line/Curve of Best Fit	2			4				
Mean, Median, Mode				3				
Normal Distribution				3				
Probability				3				
Regression Equation	2			4				
Scatter Diagrams	2			4				
Standard Deviation				3				
Weighted Average				3				
Projections				4				
TOOLS	2		2		2, 3			
Graphing Calculators	2				3			
Spreadsheets		2	1, 2	2	2			
PROCESS	1, 2, 3	1, 2, 3	1, 2	1, 2, 3, 4	1, 2, 3	1, 2, 3	1, 2	1, 2
Problem Solving	1, 2, 3	1, 2, 3	1, 2	1, 2, 3, 4	1, 2, 3	1, 2, 3	1, 2	1, 2
Reasoning and Proof	1, 2	2, 3	2	1, 2, 3, 4	2, 3	3	1	2
Communication	1, 2	2, 3	2	1, 2, 3, 4	2, 3	3	1	2
Connections	1, 2, 3	1, 2, 3	1, 2	1, 2, 3, 4	1, 2, 3	1, 2, 3	1, 2	1, 2
Representation	1, 2	2, 3	2	2, 3, 4	2, 3	3	1	2

About the Authors

 **Elizabeth Marquez** is a mathematics assessment specialist at Educational Testing Service (ETS) in Princeton, New Jersey. Elizabeth has more than thirty years of mathematics teaching experience from elementary through graduate school. She is a recipient of the Presidential Award for Excellence in Mathematics Teaching and the Princeton University Prize for Distinguished Secondary School Teaching. Elizabeth is an author of ETS's *Teacher Assistance Package Guides in Mathematics*, the *New Jersey Core Curriculum Content Standards and Frameworks*, *Mathematics Standardized Test Prep*, and for Eye on Education, with Charlotte Danielson, *A Collection of Performance Tasks and Rubrics in Mathematics*.

 **Paul Westbrook, CFP,** is President of Westbrook Financial Advisers, a fee-only financial and retirement planning firm in New Brunswick, New Jersey. Paul has spoken at financial planning and benefits conferences and has been quoted in *Money* magazine, *Fortune*, the *Wall Street Journal*, and *Barron's*. He also teaches at the business school at Rutgers University. Paul has written several books: *Word Smart for Business*, *Math Smart for Business*, and *Business Companion*. He also wrote J. K. Lasser's *New Rules for Retirement and Tax*.

To our children,
Alison, Elizabeth, and Ashley,
and
to the financial and mathematical education of all children

Cars, Cars, and More Cars

Paying for Your Wheels

When buying a used car, punch the buttons on the radio. If all the stations are rock and roll, there's a good chance the transmission is shot.
—Larry Lujack, Chicago Disc Jockey

Buying cars is one of the most engaging American activities. As such, it is a subject that should hold students' interest enough to teach them some useful math. In doing so, there are a number of applications that address the National Council of Teachers of Mathematics (NCTM) standards.

NCTM STANDARDS APPLIED IN THIS CHAPTER

Content

- *Number and Operations*. Understand meanings of operations and how they relate to one another; compute fluently and make reasonable estimates.
- *Algebra*. Understand patterns, relations, and functions; represent and analyze mathematical situations and structures using algebraic symbols; use mathematical models to represent and understand quantitative relationships.

(Continued)

(Continued)

- *Data Analysis and Probability*. Select and use appropriate statistical methods to analyze data.

Process

- Problem Solving; Reasoning and Proof; Communication; Connections; Representation

BACKGROUND: BASICS OF BUYING CARS

Cars are one of the most expensive and important things we buy. We've all done it, either buying a new or used one, buying it outright, taking a loan, or leasing. And we will continue to do it for many more years.

The particular choice of car model we make can enhance our personal image, as well as affect our pocketbook, like few purchases we make in our lives. Because the cars we buy, in total, will be one of the most expensive items we will purchase over our lifetimes, it offers a chance to save money if we're intelligent about it.

No, we're not going to talk here about how to haggle with car dealers. Instead, we're going to approach the subject from a mathematical point of view. In doing so, it is hoped that students will become more aware of the amount of money they will spend on these purchases, this year and over their lifetimes.

TEACHING EXAMPLE 1.1

Car Costs

NCTM Content Standards

Numbers and Operations; Algebra

Process Standards

Problem Solving; Reasoning and Proof; Communication; Connections; Representation

Money Applications

Students will

- Calculate the total cost of owning a car
- Calculate monthly car loan payments
- Calculate the depreciation of cars over time

Discussion and Questions

What a Deal!
$12,500

2003 Honda Civic EX Coupe 2d
ABS, Air Conditioning, Cruise
Control, Single Compact Disc, Dual
Front Airbags, FWD, Power Door
Locks, Power Steering, Power
Windows, AM/FM Stereo,
Tilt Wheel,
Only 40,000 miles,
Original Owner, Kept in Garage,
Service Records Available

Photo by Paul Westbrook.

1. Ask students how much they think the car (in the above ad) would cost them on a monthly basis, considering all possible costs, including a $10,000 loan. Give them time to think about it, jot down their estimate on a piece of paper, and explain how they reached their estimate. Have them pair-share results, reaching consensus on expenses and the monthly amount of each. Ask a few pairs to present their results to the class. Then share the following facts to see how close their estimates were to those of Edmunds, one of America's most authoritative sources of automotive information.

Monthly Auto Expenses

- *$270 per month for the car loan.* (Assuming $10,000 loan for 48 months: Range: good credit, 4% rate, and $226 a month or, if bad credit, 21% rate and $310 a month; let's say somewhere in between, about $270 a month)
- *$200 per month for auto insurance.* (On average, about $2,400 annually or $200 a month, although it could be as high as $5,000 a year or $417 a month)
- *$80 per month for maintenance.* (On average, about $80 a month—oil change, tires, etc.)
- *$107 per month for fuel.* (On average, 1,000 miles a month for teens and assuming regular gas at $2.68 per gallon and MPG of 25)
- *$7 per month for registration/license/inspection.*

SOURCE: http://www.edmunds.com.

Ask students to find the minimum and maximum monthly cost of owning a car, based on the assumptions in the list.

They should tell you that the cost is anywhere from $600 to $900 per month, a fact that will probably surprise them. Make use of that surprise to follow up with this question: What are some of the ways that the cost of a car can be reduced, short of having your parents pick up the tab? Some possible answers are the following:

- Buy a car with a clean history and a brand name known for reliability.
- Make as large a down payment as possible (at least 20%) and take a loan for at most 48 months (so you never owe more than the car is worth).
- Maintain a history of safe driving so insurance will be minimized.
- Avoid speeding, rapid acceleration, and braking. In addition to putting you and others at risk, driving carelessly can increase MPG by 5% around town and by 33% at highway speeds.
- Each car reaches its optimal fuel economy at different speeds, usually decreasing after 60 MPH.
- Remove excess weight—an extra 100 lbs in your car could reduce MPG by as much as 2%.
- Use cruise control on the highway—maintaining a constant speed saves gas.
- Keep your tires filled at proper pressure and your car engine tuned.

2. Tell students that many people take out a loan in order to buy a car and that the interest rate for the loan depends on your credit history and prevailing interest rates at the time of the loan.

Show them this table of monthly payments based on the length of the loan and the interest rate and how to apply it:

Table 1.1   Monthly Payments per $1,000

Interest Rate	2 Years (24 Months)	3 Years (36 Months)	4 Years (48 Months)	5 Years (60 Months)
6%	$44.321	$30.422	$23.485	$19.333
7%	44.773	30.877	23.946	19.801
8%	45.228	31.337	24.413	20.277

To use Table 1.1, multiply the monthly figure by the number of $1,000s borrowed. For instance, say you wanted to buy a car for $17,000, put 20% down ($3,400), and financed the remaining $13,600 with a 36-month loan at a 7% interest rate. Multiply the amount in Table 1.1 by 13.6: $30.877 times 13.6 is $419.93 (rounded to two decimal places). Therefore, the monthly payment for this car loan would be about $420. This would be the payment for each of the 36 months.

Although this is the most common method of calculating car loan payments and may be the only loan type available, some loans are different. Some have a declining monthly payment because the interest payment is recalculated as the principal of the loan is paid off.

3. Tell students that as soon as a car is driven off the dealer's lot, it declines in value. Ask them to guess how much it declines in value during the first years that you own it, then share the following table.

Table 1.2 Depreciation of a Car per Years of Use

First Year	30%
Second Year	25%
Third Year	20%
Fourth Year	15%
Fifth Year	10%

Explain that although some cars depreciate faster, or slower, it has been calculated that the value of an average car in good repair and with average mileage (about 12,000 miles a year) depreciates roughly as shown in Table 1.2. (The table assumes no major damage.)

Ask students the following:

- How much would a car be worth after one year, if it was bought for $22,000?
- How did they arrive at their answer?

Correct responses are as follows:

- $15,400.
- By calculating the amount of depreciation, 30% of $22,000, which is $6,600, and then subtracting it from $22,000 or, in just one step, taking 70% of $22,000, recognizing that a 30% reduction means a 70% value.

Now ask students the following:

- How much is the car worth after 2 years?
- How did they arrive at their answer?

Correct responses are as follows:

- $11,550.
- By calculating the amount of depreciation, 25% of $15,400, which is $3,850, and then subtracting it from $15,400 or, in just one step, taking 75% of $15,400, recognizing that a 25% reduction means a 75% value.

Ask students, in just one step, to find the value of the car after 3 years. They should tell you that the value is $9,240, and their one step was to take 80% of $11,550.

Challenge students to find, in just one step, the present value of a 3-year-old car that was purchased for $30,000 assuming normal depreciation, normal wear and tear, and average mileage. Be sure to give them time to try this. The one step is

$$\$12,600 = \$30,000(0.70)(0.75)(0.80).$$

Ask students how they got the factors of 0.70, 0.75, and 0.80 and then rewrite the one step as

$$\$12,600 = \$30,000(1 - 0.30)(1 - 0.25)(1 - 0.20).$$

Finally, ask them to generalize their one step by letting

V = present value
P = purchase price
d_n = depreciation percent in the nth year

The generalization is

$$V = P(1 - d_1)(1 - d_2)...(1 - d_n).$$

Practice

1. If you took out a car loan for $10,000 for 4 years at 8%, what would the monthly payments be?

2. If someone gets an $8,000 car loan at 7% interest for 3 years, what would the monthly payment for that loan be?

3. Calculate the value after 5 years of depreciation of a car purchased for $30,000.

4. Using the following depreciation schedule, which is slightly higher than the standard table, of 35%, 30%, 25%, 20%, and 15%, calculate the value of a car after 5 years of use and with an original price of $40,000.

5. If a 2-year-old car is presently valued at $10,000, approximate its original purchase price based on the information in Table 1.2 and based on the schedule given in the preceding problem.

Practice Answers

1. $244.13 (24.413 times 10 equals $244.13).

2. $247.02 (30.877 times 8 equals $247.02).

3. $9,639 ($30,000 times .7 times .75 times .8 times .85 times .9 equals $9,639).

4. $9,282 ($40,000 times .65 times .7 times .75 times .8 times .85 equals $9,282).

5. $19,048 (solve $10,000 = $P(0.7)(0.75)$); $21,978 (solve $10,000 = P(0.65)(0.7)$).

Project

Have the students go to the Edmunds Web site (www.edmunds.com) to find the monthly cost of owning, using, and maintaining their favorite car. Also, have them compare that cost to the cost if they lived in a different U.S. state.

TEACHING EXAMPLE 1.2

MPG Plus

NCTM Content Standards

Numbers and Operations; Algebra; Data Analysis and Probability

Process Standards

Problem Solving; Reasoning and Proof; Communication; Connections; Representation

Money Applications

Students will

- Project lifetime costs of buying cars
- Calculate the effect of MPG (miles per gallon) on car costs
- Use regression and correlation to project gas mileage at various speeds

Discussion and Questions

Two important aspects of buying and owning cars are the following:

- Understanding just how much we will spend over our lifetimes on cars
- Understanding the relationship between how fast we drive and MPG

1. Students might not appreciate that a huge amount of their money will go toward the cars they buy over their lifetimes. How many cars each student will buy (or lease) will depend on factors such as their desire to have the latest and best model or how much they would like to save on this expense. It will not be uncommon to buy 12 or more cars over a lifetime.

Assuming they buy 12 cars over their lifetimes and working in today's dollars, ask students the difference between buying 12 cars at $18,000 each as opposed to 12 cars at $35,000 each.

Use the following formula:

$$TC = Cost \times Number,$$

where

TC = the total cost
$Cost$ = the cost of one car
$Number$ = the number of cars

We can then solve the formula for cars that cost $18,000 and $35,000:

$$TC = Cost \times Number$$
$$TC = \$18,000 \times 12$$
$$TC = \$216,000$$

or,

$$TC = \$35,000 \times 12$$
$$TC = \$420,000$$

That is, they would save $204,000 over their lifetimes. This may surprise most students. However, there are other considerations, such as fuel efficiency, safety features, and repair costs, in deciding how much to spend on a car.

2. Let's look at MPG, an important ratio that tells you how many miles you can drive, on average, city or highway, on 1 gallon of gasoline. For instance, suppose that you own a car that gets 28 MPG in highway driving and that the fuel tank holds 13.2 gallons. How far can you travel on that amount of gas, assuming you're driving only on the highway?

To get that answer, students can set up the following proportion and cross-multiply to solve

$$\frac{x \text{ miles}}{13.2 \text{ gallons}} = \frac{28 \text{ miles}}{1 \text{ gallon}} \Rightarrow x = 369.6.$$

Now ask students to find the city MPG for the same car if a tank lasts for only 300 miles of city driving.

Once again, students can solve by using a proportion:

$$\frac{300 \text{ miles}}{13.2 \text{ gallons}} = \frac{x \text{ miles}}{1 \text{ gallon}} \Rightarrow x \approx 22.7.$$

Finally, ask students to calculate the cost of gas if driving from New York City to Los Angeles, about 2,790 miles, in that same car if 20% of the drive is city driving. Since the price of gas varies across the country, have students use the average cost per gallon and assume that average is $2.80/gal (to be current, the average cost of fuel can be found on the Internet at www.fueleconomy.gov or similar sites).

Have them explain their work.

Using the figures above, they should tell you that the cost of gas for the entire trip is $289.52:

- First, students should determine how many gallons of gas are needed for city driving and how many are needed for highway driving. Since the total trip is 2,790 miles and 20% of it is city driving, then

$$0.20 \times 2,790 \text{ miles} = 558 \text{ miles is the } city \text{ distance, and}$$
$$2,790 - 558 = 2,232 \text{ miles is the } highway \text{ distance.}$$

- Second, they should determine how many gallons of gas are needed to travel those distances. Since 1 gallon of gas lasts 23.7 miles in the city but 28 miles on the highway, the number of gallons needed for city driving is

$$\frac{558 \text{ miles}}{22.7 \frac{\text{miles}}{\text{gallon}}} \approx 24.6 \text{ gallons and } \frac{2{,}232 \text{ miles}}{28 \frac{\text{miles}}{\text{gallon}}} \approx 79.7 \text{ gallons.}$$

- Finally, they should multiply the total gallons by the cost, $2.80 per gallon:

$$(24.6 \text{ gallons} + 79.9 \text{ gallons}) \times \frac{\$2.80}{\text{gallon}} = \$292.60.$$

Practice

(Assume today's costs for all these problems—future value problems will be used in the next chapter.)

1. Have students calculate how much they would spend throughout their lives on car purchases if they buy a $15,000 car every 5 years and every 10 years. Use present-day dollars and assume a 50-year period.

2. Have students calculate how much they would spend throughout their lives if they would buy more expensive cars of $30,000 every 5 years and every 10 years. Use present-day dollars and assume a 50-year period.

3. Have students calculate how much they would save throughout their lives if they bought only 5 cars at $15,000 versus 10 cars at $30,000.

4. Have students construct a table showing the total lifetime outlays of $15,000, $22,000, and $30,000 cars every 5 and 10 years, assuming a 50-year period.

5. Assuming you drive 1,000 miles a month, pay $2.58 per gallon, and get 28 MPG, calculate how much you would save each month if you

   - Found a gas station that charged 10 cents less per gallon
   - Drove smart enough to increase your present MPG of 28 by 20%

Practice Answers

1. $150,000 and $75,000 ($15,000 times 10 cars equals $150,000; $15,000 times 5 cars equals $75,000).

2. $300,000 and $150,000 ($30,000 times 10 cars equals $300,000; $30,000 times 5 cars equals $150,000).

3. $225,000 ($30,000 times 10 cars equals $300,000; $15,000 times 5 cars equals $75,000; $300,000 minus $75,000 equals $225,000).

4. See the following table:

Total Lifetime Outlay of Cars		
Cost of One Car	Every 5 Years	Every 10 Years
$15,000	$150,000	$75,000
22,000	220,000	110,000
30,000	300,000	150,000

5. At an MPG of 28, we use a proportion to get the gallons of gas needed to go 1,000 miles:

$$\frac{28 \text{ miles}}{\text{gallon}} = \frac{1,000 \text{ miles}}{x \text{ gallon}} \Rightarrow x \approx 35.7 \text{ gallons}.$$

So, the old cost is

$$\text{Cost}_{\text{new}} = \frac{\$2.58}{\text{gallon}} \times 35.7 \text{ gallon} = \$92.11.$$

The new MPG is 120% of 28 or 33.6 miles per gallon. To find the gallons needed to go 1,000 miles, we can use a proportion:

$$\frac{33.6 \text{ miles}}{\text{gallon}} = \frac{1,000 \text{ miles}}{x \text{ gallon}}$$
$$x \approx 29.8$$

The cost per gallon is $2.58 − $.10 = $2.48. So, total cost is now

$$\text{Cost}_{\text{new}} = \frac{\$2.48}{\text{gallon}} \times 29.8 \text{ gallon} = \$73.90.$$

So, smart shopping and driving saved $92.11 − $73.90 = $18.21 a month. Enough for a couple of movie tickets—not bad!

Extension

Let's talk about the relationship between speed and gas mileage. Every car has a speed limit at which it gets its best gas mileage. For most cars, that optimal speed does not exceed 60 MPH.

Suppose the following data were collected on the speed and gas mileage of your car as follows:

MPH	5	10	15	20	25	30	35	40	45	50	55	60	65
MPG	10	15	23	25	27	28	29	30	31	31.5	30	28.5	27

Ask students, "At what speed does your car get its best gas mileage?" They should tell you it gets its best mileage at about 50 MPH.

Now ask them to project the gas mileage at 75 MPH. Here is one way they can make a good projection. Have them use their graphing calculators to graph speed versus MPG. Lists and a graph should look as shown below:

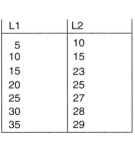

L1	L2
5	10
10	15
15	23
20	25
25	27
30	28
35	29

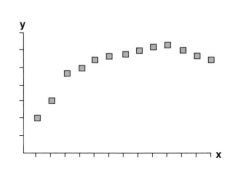

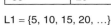
L1 = {5, 10, 15, 20, …}

Ask the students:

1. if a line of best fit would be the best model for these data and, if not,

2. to suggest another model.

They should tell you that the points look like they would fit a parabola better than a line. Students should then test to see which actually does provide the better fit by performing the correlation diagnostics.

They should get the results pictured below:

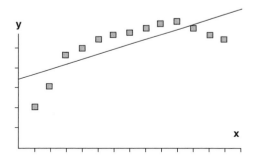

Lin Reg
  y = ax+b
  a = .2494505495
  b = 17.03846154
  r^2 = .5721947699
  r = .7564355689

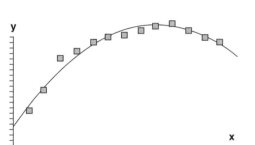

Quad Reg
  y = ax^2+bx+c
  a = −.0124675325
  b = 1.122177822
  c = 6.129370629
  R^2 = .965263652

The correlation diagnostics of r^2 and R^2 indicate that the parabola is the better fit since R^2 is closer to 1 than r^2. Although r^2 and R^2 are calculated differently, their values can be compared to determine which regression fits the data better. Be sure students know that the closer r^2 or R^2 is to 1, the better the fit.

So, we will use the parabola to project gas mileage at 75 MPH by finding $y(75)$. Students should calculate $y(75)$, obtaining the answer of about 20.2 MPG.

This is worse than the MPG at 15 MPH! Cars do not operate efficiently at low as well as high speeds. So, if you want to save money, do your highway driving at the speed at which you get the most miles to the gallon.

Projects

1. Ask the students to devise and apply a method for determining the average MPG that their car or the family car gets. After they have had time to apply their method, have them present their method and the results of its application to the class. (Note: One simple method is to fill up the tank and zero the trip meter in their car and then, when they next get gas, fill up the tank again and record the number of gallons purchased as well as the reading on the trip meter. The reading on the trip meter divided by the number of gallons is the miles per gallon.)

2. Ask students to use the quadratic regression model above to project the mileage for 80, 85, and 90 MPH.

3. Based on the example above and current prices for regular gas, calculate the money you would save per mile traveling at 55 rather than 70 MPH.

4. Find a regression model with a high correlation for the following data and to use it to project mileage for 75, 80, and 85 MPG.

MPH	10	15	20	25	30	35	40	45	50	55	60	65	70
MPG	18	25	28	29.5	31	33.8	35	37.5	39	40.3	42	39	36

TEACHING EXAMPLE 1.3

Buy or Lease

NCTM Content Standards

Numbers and Operations

Process Standards

Problem Solving; Connections

Money Applications

Students will

- Compare buying versus leasing a car

Discussion and Questions

Leasing a car is essentially renting it—not for just a weekend or a week but for 3 or 4 years!

Why is it enticing? Because the actual monthly payments during the lease period are less than if you took out a car loan to pay for it. After all, when you lease, you only are renting, not buying.

Let's take an example:

If you bought a car priced at $25,000 and you put 20% down ($5,000), you would need to finance $20,000. If you took out a loan for 4 years at 7%, your monthly payments for the 4 years would be about $480 (see Table 1.1). If you continue to own the car thereafter, then there would be no monthly payments (although your maintenance costs could increase).

On the other hand, if you leased the same car, after you paid nonrefundable fee(s), your monthly payments for 4 years could be about $330. This would be $150 less a month. But after 4 years, you would not own the car and, in fact, would have to buy or lease another car. That's why the payments are less.

To show an example where buying a car is better financially, consider the following situation:

Buy a car and keep it for 8 years versus lease a car for 4 years and then lease another one for another 4 years.

The cost of buying this car would be $480 (estimated monthly loan payments) times 12 months times 4 years, or a total of $23,040.

The cost of leasing 2 cars over 8 years would be $330 times 12 months times 8 years, or a total of $31,680 (assuming that the lease on the second car would be the same as the first and that you did not pay any fee).

In this example, leasing would cost $8,640 more!

Leasing also comes with several potential negative surprises. First, if you drive a leased car more than the "normal" mileage (often 10,000 to 15,000 a year), then you will have to pay extra when you finish the lease. Second, if the car has any dings or dents, you will have to pay extra for them when the lease is up. Third, if you have damage to the car, the insurance will pay the dealer (who owns the car), but often it is not enough to cover the total amount of the damage, so you may have to pay the difference.

Practice

1. Using the example above about leasing, calculate the percentage of the price of the car that each monthly payment equals.

2. Using the percent calculated in your answer to Question 1, calculate the monthly lease payments for a car worth $30,000.

3. Calculate the savings if you bought a car for $18,000, paid 20% down, and took out a 4-year loan for 7% versus leasing the same car. Assume that you would keep the car you bought for 8 years versus leasing 2 cars over the 8 years. Also assume the same percentage for the answer in Question 1.

Practice Answers

1. The monthly payment is 1.32% of the price. (Price of the car is $25,000 and the monthly lease payments are $330; $330 divided by $25,000 equals .0132, or 1.32%.)

2. $396 a month ($30,000 times 1.32% (0.0132) equals $396).

3. $6,718 (the down payment of 20% on $18,000 equals $3,600, and thus the amount that would need to be financed would be $14,400. Table 1.1 shows the amount of $23.946 times 14.4 equals $344.82, $344.82 times 12 times 4 equals $16,551; leasing would cost 1.32% of $18,000 equals $237.60, $237.60 times 12 times 8 equals $22,810; difference between $22,810 minus $16,551 equals $6,259).

2

Savings

Reality Check and the Difference Between Needs and Wants

How can I be out of money when I still have checks in my checkbook?
—Clueless Nonsaver

Saving money is a key aspect of one's personal finance and, as such, offers an opportunity to not only weave math into this subject but also to offer useful living strategies for students. There are a number of applications that address the National Council of Teachers of Mathematics (NCTM) standards.

NCTM STANDARDS APPLIED IN THIS CHAPTER

Content

- *Number and Operations.* Understand meanings of operations and how they relate to one another; compute fluently and make reasonable estimates.
- *Algebra.* Understand patterns, relations, and functions; represent and analyze mathematical situations and structures using algebraic symbols; use mathematical models to represent and understand quantitative relationships; analyze change in various contexts.

Process

- Problem Solving; Reasoning and Proof; Communication; Connections; Representation

BACKGROUND: BASICS OF SAVINGS

Why Is Saving Money Important?

Savings involves putting money aside today so you have enough to buy things later. For instance, if you want to buy a car, you will usually need to put down a certain amount of money, even if you finance it. And, later in life, if you buy a house, often a down payment of 25% of its value is required up front (although sometimes a lesser amount is okay).

Much later in life, you may need to pay for college or other education for your children. Finally, when you reach an older age, you would like a comfortable retirement. All these things have one thing in common: You've had to save (and invest) money during your work life.

Difference Between Needs and Wants Is Critical

Spending and saving are opposite sides of the equation. In fact, you will try to balance these two for the rest of your life, like a teeter-totter. The key is to distinguish between *needs* and *wants*. Needs are the necessities of life, like paying the rent and buying groceries. Wants are what you would like, desires such as wide-screen TVs, extra jewelry, and extra toys that clutter a child's room. Often, however, people don't distinguish between the two and view their desired wants as necessities. The result: They never seem to have any money left over for savings.

Many years ago, the Federal Reserve did a study that showed that how you handled money when you were a teenager is likely how you will handle money throughout your life. That is, if you were a spender then, you'll probably be a spender for the rest of your life. On the other hand, if you were a saver, then you'll naturally save money. Married couples, of course, can have a mixture, one spender and one saver. Then, tensions can arise as each spouse pulls in the opposite direction. The answer is generally to agree on specific goals to attain.

If, however, both are spenders, then they need to be wary because there is no one spouse to put the brakes on spending. If both are savers, on the other hand, then they will probably feel comfortable saving enough money for their future needs.

What's the Problem With Savings?

Saving is that difficult activity of doing a little at a time, for instance, saving $100 a month, month after month. Sometimes it can feel painful, and often it's boring. Spending money, on the other hand, is fun. It's an experience we try to have as often as possible. This is why so many people end up with credit card debt, the math of which is covered in the next chapter.

The purpose of savings is more than just paying for specific things later on, although that is its main purpose. It is also the ability to weather financial difficulties when they unexpectedly strike. A person may find that he or she is suddenly out of work, or might be disabled for a period of time and can't work, among other financial difficulties. Having some savings, then, can provide a cushion to fall back on in bad times.

TEACHING EXAMPLE 2.1

Budgets and Savings

NCTM Content Standards

Numbers and Operations; Algebra

Process Standards

Problem Solving; Connections

Money Applications

Students will

- Calculate amount of savings that can be accumulated over time
- Calculate how much a person needs to save to meet an objective
- Calculate how much a person can save using a budget

Discussion and Questions

Engage students by posing the following situation.

Suppose you have a Monday-through-Friday job, with 2 weeks of vacation, and you decide to save money by putting $2 into a jar each working day. If no other money goes into the jar and no money comes out, how much would be in the jar at the end of 5 years?

Students should tell you that $2,500 would be in their jar at the end of 5 years because they save $10 per week for 50 weeks each year for 5 years. That is,

$$\frac{\$10}{\text{week}} \times \frac{50 \text{ weeks}}{\text{year}} \times 5 \text{ years} = \$2,500.$$

Then ask students to do the following:

Determine how much would be in the jar if you put $5 into the jar each workday for 7 years.

Photo by Paul Westbrook.

Answer: $8,750 because

$$\frac{\$25}{\text{week}} \times \frac{50 \text{ weeks}}{\text{year}} \times 7 \text{ years} = \$8,750.$$

Write a formula for the amount of money, *A*, that would be in the jar if you put *m* dollars into the jar each workday for *n* years.

Answer: $250*mn* because

$$\frac{\$m \times 5}{\text{week}} \times \frac{50 \text{ weeks}}{\text{weeks}} \times n \text{ years} = \$250mn.$$

Write the formula you would use if you put *m* dollars into the jar *d* days a week each week for *n* years.

Answer: $52*mdn* because

$$\frac{\$m \times d}{\text{week}} \times \frac{52\,\text{weeks}}{\text{year}} \times n \text{ years} = \$52mdn.$$

Now ask students to do the following:

Give a plan for having $3,000 in the jar after 2 years. Assume that you put the same amount into the jar each week for 50 weeks of the year with no withdrawals.

Answer: There are many possible answers—to enhance number sense, challenge students to give several answers!

For example, one answer is $5/day for 6 days/week since

$$\frac{\$5 \times 6}{\text{week}} \times \frac{50\,\text{weeks}}{\text{year}} \times 2 \text{ years} = \$3,000.$$

Another answer is $7.50/day for 4 days/week since

$$\frac{\$15 \times 2}{\text{week}} \times \frac{50\,\text{weeks}}{\text{year}} \times 2 \text{ years} = \$3,000.$$

Now engage the students by asking them the fundamental question:

How do people find the money to save and still be able to pay for their needs and some wants?

The answer is usually from a budget! This may seem obvious, but many people, regardless of how smart they are or how much they earn in their jobs, do not budget and end up mired in debt.

Share the following information with students—the rate of savings has been on a steady decline for the past 2 decades, and in 2005, the rate was actually negative! This is the first time since 1933. That means that Americans spent all of their incomes, plus withdrew money from previous savings or increased their debt.

Present students with this example (Table 2.1) of a single person's budget, income, and expenses.

Ask students the following:

If this person saved all of the money that is available to save each month, how much will be saved at the end of 3 years?

Answer: $12,600 because

$$\frac{\$350}{\text{month}} \times \frac{12\,\text{months}}{\text{year}} \times 3 \text{ years} = \$12,600.$$

(This assumes no interest on the savings, which will be covered in the next teaching example.)

Table 2.1 Budget: Single Person

	Monthly	*Annually*
Income	**$2,917**	**$35,000**
Expenses		
Rent	$850	$10,200
Utilities	83	996
Telephone	80	960
Groceries	350	4,200
Clothing	85	1,020
Eating Out	150	1,800
Car Loan	317	3,804
Gas and Maintenance	64	768
Insurances	108	1,296
Taxes	375	4,500
Miscellaneous	105	1,260
Available to Save	350	4,200
Total	**$2,917**	**$35,000 rounded**

Table 2.2 Budget: Married Couple

	Monthly	*Annually*
Income	**$6,083**	**$73,000**
Expenses		
Mortgage	$1,664	$19,968
Real Estate Taxes	500	6,000
Utilities	225	2,700
Telephone	100	1,200
Groceries	600	7,200
Clothing	110	1,320
Eating Out	200	2,400
Car Loan	425	5,100
Gas and Maintenance	95	1,140
Insurances	225	2,700
Taxes	1,200	14,400
Entertainment	200	2,400
Miscellaneous	100	1,200
Available to Save	436	5,232
Total	**$6,083**	**$73,000 rounded**

Practice

Review the budgets above (Table 2.2) and then answer the questions that follow.

1. How much will this couple save over 3 years if they save the entire $436 per month?

2. What percent of their monthly salaries is available for savings each month?

3. How might this couple change their budget so that they can increase the amount of their savings to 10% per month? How much would they save each month after the change?

4. How much more could the single person save if her utilities and rent were shared equally by an apartment mate? What percent of her income could then be saved?

Practice Answers

1. $15,696 since

$$\frac{\$436}{month} \times \frac{12 \text{ months}}{year} \times 3 \text{ years} = \$15,696.$$

2. 13.75% since

$$\frac{part}{whole} = \frac{\$436}{\$6,080} = .0717, \text{ or about } 7\%.$$

3. There are many possible ways to increase their savings by 10% or about $608/mth. An example of ways to do this is to reduce the money they spend eating out to $100/mth and reduce their utility bills by $20 by "turning off the juice when not in use" coupled with reducing their entertainment costs by $52.

4. She could now save $466.50 more a month for a total savings of $816.50 or almost 30% of her income.

Projects

1. Write a budget for yourself; include all income—from allowance, part-time job, gifts, and so on—and any expenses for which you may be responsible. Do you have money to save? How might you save more? Where do you keep (invest) the money that you save? Chapter 4 covers investing.

2. Explain the adage, "Invest early and invest often."

TEACHING EXAMPLE 2.2

Future Value: A Geometric Sequence

NCTM Content Standards

Numbers and Operations; Algebra

Process Standards

Problem Solving; Reasoning and Proof; Communication; Connections; Representation

Money Applications

Students will

- Develop the formula for future value using a geometric sequence
- Apply the future value formula to determine future value, interest, and time

Discussion and Questions

Tell students that instead of just putting money in a jar (or piggybank), they can put it in a bank where it can earn interest. That is, their savings will earn additional savings!

When interest earned is added to the principal at stated periods—say, annually, semiannually, or quarterly—the interest is said to be *compounded*. Compounded means that interest is earned on interest during the year. If *PV (present value)* is the original principal, r the interest rate per year, and n is the number of years, then:

$$FV = PV(1+r)^n,$$

where

$FV =$ future value
$PV =$ present value
$r =$ rate of interest (or investment)
$n =$ number of years

To develop this formula, we can see that the interest earned at the end of the first year is:

$$PV \times r.$$

Thus, the total amount of money at the end of the first year is

$$PV + PV \times r \quad \text{or} \quad PV(1+r) \text{ (distributive law)}.$$

The new principal, then, at the end of a year is simply $1+r$ times the principal at the beginning of the year. So, after n successive years, FV is

$$FV = PV(1+r)^n.$$

To understand the nature of r, as a percent, let us compare the decimal version to the actual percent. Suppose $r = 5\%$ and compounding is done annually (once a year); then, to calculate with r, we must convert it to its decimal form .05, as in

$$FV = PV(1 + .05)^n.$$

So, when we use r, we mean the decimal version.

To help students understand the development of our basic formula, ask students the following question:

Suppose that you are able to save \$3,000 a year and can earn 6% interest on your money. How much will be in the account after 5 years? How much would you have after n years?

Work with the students to construct a table such as the one that is completed below. Give them time to recognize the pattern and to express it in general form as shown in the nth row.

End of Year	Amount in Account (Principal + Interest)	Amount in Account Factored Using Distributive Law Then Simplified
1	$3,000 + 3,000(.06)$	$3,000(1 + .06) = 3,000(1.06) = \$3,180$
2	$3,000(1.06) + 3,000(1.06)(.06)$	$3,000(1.06)(1 + .06) = 3,000(1.06)^2 = \$3,370.80$
3	$3,000(1.06)^2 + 3,000(1.06)^2(.06)$	$3,000(1.06)^2(1 + .06) = 3,000(1.06)^3 = \$3,573.05$
4	$3,000(1.06)^3 + 3,000(1.06)^3(.06)$	$3,000(1.06)^3(1 + .06) = 3,000(1.06)^4 = \$3,787.43$
5	$3,000(1.06)^4 + 3,000(1.06)^4(.06)$	$3,000(1.06)^4(1 + .06) = 3,000(1.06)^5 = \$4,014.68$
$\vdots$	$\vdots$	$\vdots$
n	$3,000(1.06)^{n-1} + 3,000(1.06)^{n-1}(.06)$	$3,000(1.06)^{n-1}(1 + .06) = 3,000(1.06)^n$

Students should see that the pattern in the table is a geometric sequence, with a common ratio of 1.06.

Answer: After 5 years, you have \$4,015 (rounded), calculated as

$$\$3,000(1 + .06)^5 = \$4,015.$$

After n years, $\$3,000(1 + .06)^n$.

Now ask students how their money would grow if it were compounded *monthly* (interest earning interest each and every month).

How would our formula be modified?

$$FV = PV\left(1 + \frac{r}{12}\right)^{n \times 12}.$$

The annual interest rate r is divided by 12, the number of compounding periods in one year, and the number of years n is multiplied by 12 to get the total number of compounding periods.

How would our formula be written if the money would be compounded quarterly (interest earning interest four times a year)?

$$FV = PV\left(1 + \frac{r}{4}\right)^{n \times 4}.$$

How would our formula be written if the compounding period is k times per year?

$$FV = PV\left(1 + \frac{r}{k}\right)^{n \times k}$$

Now ask the students the following:

How can we find either the rate of interest, r, or the number of years, n, using the general formula?

Solving for r in our basic formula of $FV = PV(1 + r)^n$, we obtain

$$r = \left(\frac{FV}{PV}\right)^{\frac{1}{n}} - 1 \text{ or, } r = \sqrt[n]{\frac{FV}{PV}} - 1.$$

Solving for n in our basic formula of $FV = PV(1 + r)^n$, we obtain

$$n = \log\frac{FV}{PV} \text{ divided by } \log(1 + r).$$

(The natural log, ln, can also be used to solve for n as can any $\log_b$ where $b > 0$.)

Practice

1. Calculate the future value of $1,000 earning an annual interest rate of 6% after 10 years, if compounded:
   a. annually
   b. semiannually
   c. quarterly
   d. monthly
   e. daily

2. Calculate the value of $1,000 in 10 years if compounding is annual and if the interest rate is
   a. 6%
   b. 6.5%
   c. 7%
   d. 7.5%
   e. 8%

3. Use a spreadsheet to show the future value of $1,000 in 10 years for each of the following compoundings: annual, semiannual, quarterly, monthly, and daily, calculated at each of the following interest rates: 4.5%, 5.0%, 5.5%, 6%, 6.5%, 7%, 7.5%, 8%, 8.5%, 9%, 9.5%, and 10%.

4. Which has a greater impact, an increase in interest rate or number of compoundings? Explain.

5. How long would you have to wait until a $1,000 deposit doubled in value, assuming your money earned 6% interest compounded annually?

6. Find the annual interest rate your money would have to earn in order for it to quadruple in 20 years.

7. The "rule of 72" is a rule of thumb that allows you to approximate the time it will take for money to double at a given interest rate. It is called the rule of 72 because at 10% interest, money will double every 7.2 years. To use the rule, divide the annual interest into 72. For example, if you get 4% annual interest, your money will double in about $\frac{72}{4} = 18$ years. Apply the rule of 72 to Problem 5 and compare results.

8. Can the rule of 72 be applied to Problem 6?

9. Find the annual interest rate your money would have to earn in order for it to triple in 15 years.

Practice Answers

1. Solving for $1,000(1 + \frac{.06}{p})^{10 \times p}$ for $p = 1, 2, 4, 12, 365$:
   a. $1,790.85
   b. $1,806.11
   c. $1,814.02
   d. $1,819.40
   e. $1,822.03

2. Solving for $1,000(1 + r)^{10}$ for $r = 6, 6.5, 7, 7.5, 8$:
   a. $1,790.85
   b. $1,877.14
   c. $1,967.15
   d. $2,061.03
   e. $2,158.92

3.

	A	B	C	D	E	F	G
1		*Future Value in 10 years of a Present Value Investment of $1,000:*					
2							
3			Number of Compoundings Per Year				
4			1	2	4	12	365
5		Interest					
6		Rate					
7		4.50%	$1,552.97	$1,560.51	$1,564.38	$1,566.99	$1,568.27
8		5.00%	$1,628.89	$1,638.62	$1,643.62	$1,647.01	$1,648.66
9		5.50%	$1,708.14	$1,720.43	$1,726.77	$1,731.08	$1,733.18
10		6.00%	$1,790.85	$1,806.11	$1,814.02	$1,819.40	$1,822.03
11		6.50%	$1,877.14	$1,895.84	$1,905.56	$1,912.18	$1,915.43
12		7.00%	$1,967.15	$1,989.79	$2,001.60	$2,009.66	$2,013.62
13		7.50%	$2,061.03	$2,088.15	$2,102.35	$2,112.06	$2,116.84
14		8.00%	$2,158.92	$2,191.12	$2,208.04	$2,219.64	$2,225.35
15		8.50%	$2,260.98	$2,298.91	$2,318.90	$2,332.65	$2,339.42
16		9.00%	$2,367.36	$2,411.71	$2,435.19	$2,451.36	$2,459.33
17		9.50%	$2,478.23	$2,529.77	$2,557.15	$2,576.06	$2,585.39
18		10.00%	$2,593.74	$2,653.30	$2,685.06	$2,707.04	$2,717.91

Suggestion 1: Format cells B7 to B18 to percentage.
Suggestion 2: Use the formula =1000*(1 + $B$7/C4)^(10*C4) in cell number C7 and copy it across to G7. The dollar signs in $B$7 keep B7 constant as the interest rate, so just the compoundings will

vary. Move the formula down to C8, changing \$B\$7 to \$B\$8. Then copy it across to G8. Continue in similar fashion to complete the sheet. Note that the formula is simply the spreadsheet version of

$$FV = PV\left(1 + \frac{r}{k}\right)^{n \times k},$$

with

$$PV = \$1{,}000$$
$$r = \$B\$7$$
$$k = C4$$
$$n = 10$$

4. An increase in interest rate usually has the greater impact, as can be seen in the last three problems.

5. About 12 years. Solving for n in our basic formula of $\$2{,}000 = \$1{,}000(1 + .06)^n$, we obtain,

$$n = \log \frac{\$2{,}000}{\$1{,}000} \text{ divided by } \log(1 + .06)$$

$$n = \log 2 \text{ divided by } \log 1.06$$

$$n \approx 11.9 \text{ years}$$

(Natural logs could also be used to solve for n.)

6. About 7%. Since your money quadruples, substitute 4 for FV and 1 for PV in our basic formula. Solving for n,

$$4 = (1 + r)^{20} \rightarrow \sqrt[20]{4} - 1 = r \rightarrow \approx 0.07, \text{ or } 7\%.$$

7. About 12 years. Using the rule of 72, at 6% annually, your money will double in about $\frac{72}{6} = 12$ years.

8. Yes. The rule of 72 can be applied to Problem 6 since quadrupling is the same as doubling twice. So, our money should quadruple in about 20 years (2 times 10 years equals 20 years).

9. Solving for r, we get 7.6%:

$$3PV = PV(1 + r)^{15} \rightarrow 3 = (1 + r)^{15} \rightarrow \sqrt[15]{3} = 1 + r \approx 0.076 = 7.6\%.$$

Project

1. Find out how much interest your local banks are paying on certificates of deposit (CDs) and savings accounts, and then answer the following questions:
   a. What is the best deal you can get on a CD for 1 and 2 years?
   b. Do your local banks offer CDs with variable interest rates?
   c. What are the advantages and disadvantages of CDs compared to savings accounts?
   d. How important is the maturity date on a CD?

2. Have students perform the step-by-step algebraic transformations, starting with the basic *FV* formula, to solve for *r* and *n*.

Extension

We have used the standard formula for future and present value, that is,

$$FV = PV(1+r)^n \text{ and } PV = \frac{FV}{(1+r)^n}.$$

However, sometimes a similar formula is used that contains the irrational number of *e*. This formula is

$$FV = e^{rt},$$

where

$e =$ the constant 2.718 . . .
$r =$ the rate of interest or investment
$t =$ the time or years of the investment

There is a difference between our standard basic formula and this *e* formula. The *e* formula assumes "continuous" compounding of interest. But, in fact, no bank or investment company gives this type of interest, so the results of the formula are slightly incorrect if applied to discrete compounding. However, the *e* formula has an advantage in calculus applications.

In fact, it is because of this advantage of ease that the *e* formula is sometimes used. To illustrate how the two formulas give slightly different results, let's solve each for the following: the future value in 20 years of an investment with a present value of $1,000 and an annual rate of interest of 8%.

Basic Formula

$$FV = PV(1+r)^n$$
$$FV = \$1,000(1+.08)^{20}$$
$$FV = \$4,660.96$$

e Formula

$$FV = 1,000e^{rt}$$
$$FV = 1,000e^{1.6}$$
$$FV = \$4,953.03$$

In other words, the *e* formula is greater by about $300. If the number of years were greater than the 20 years in this example, the difference would be greater.

Project

Have the students create a table with varying interest rates and number of years using the traditional and *e* formulas to compare the results.

TEACHING EXAMPLE 2.3

Annuities: A Geometric Series

NCTM Content Standards

Numbers and Operations; Algebra

Process Standards

Problem Solving; Reasoning and Proof; Communication; Connections; Representation

Money Applications

Students will

- Calculate future values and present values of annuities
- Derive formulas for calculation of future and present value of annuities using a geometric series
- Calculate how much a person needs to save to meet an objective

Discussion and Questions

Engage students by asking them what an annuity is. You may get several different answers.

Tell students that an annuity is a series of fixed equal payments made over a specified period of time. These are either payments you receive or payments you provide. There are two types of basic annuities—*ordinary annuities* and *annuities due. Ordinary annuities* are those for which payments are made (or received) at the "end" of each period, such as investments to Individual Retirement Accounts (IRAs). *Annuities due* are those for which payments are made (or received) at the "beginning" of each period, such as rent, loans, and pension payments.

Then ask students the following:

Suppose that your uncle deposits $2,000 in an account for you each December 31 for the next 5 years and that the money earns 6% per year. How much will be in that account at the end of 5 years, assuming no withdrawals?

Answer: Since the payment is made at the end of the year, this is an ordinary annuity. Using the math developed in Teaching Activity 2.2, we can calculate the future value of this annuity by calculating the future value of each annual deposit, $FV = PV(1 + r)^n$, and then sum all those individual future values to get the total of the annuity at the end of 5 years. Note the following table:

End of Year	Amount of Deposit	Number of Years Earning Interest	Future Value (Value at the End of 5 Years)
1	$2,000	4	$2,000(1.06)^4 = $2,524.76
2	$2,000	3	$2,000(1.06)^3 = $2,382.03
3	$2,000	2	$2,000(1.06)^2 = $2,247.20
4	$2,000	1	$2,000(1.06)^1 = $2,120.00
5	$2,000	0	$2,000(1.06)^0 = $2,000.00

$$\textbf{Total} \text{ on December 31 of the fifth year} = \$11,274.18$$

Note that because investments are made at the end of each year, the last deposit earns no interest, and the first deposit is compounded only four times, rather than five.

The total value at the end of the fifth year is the sum of the last column:

$$\$2,000(1.06)^4 + \$2,000(1.06)^3 + \$2,000(1.06)^2$$
$$+ \$2,000(1.06) + \$2,000, \text{ or } \$11,274.18.$$

Ask the students if they recognize this type of sum.

It's a *geometric series* with $a = \$2,000$ and $x = 1.06$, the common ratio. Remembering that the sum of a geometric series is

$$a + ax + ax^2 + \cdots + ax^{n-1} = \frac{a(x^n - 1)}{x - 1},$$

the total future value then is:

$$\frac{\$2,000(1.06^5 - 1)}{1.06 - 1} = \$11,274.19.$$

There is a slight difference between this amount and the amount in the table. This is due to rounding in the table to the nearest cent at the end of each year.

Now ask the students the following:

Suppose that your uncle deposited the money on January 1 of each year for 5 years instead of at the end of the year on December 31. The investment is now an *annuity due* because the payment is made at the *beginning* of each interest period. How much will be in this account at the end of 5 years, assuming no withdrawals?

Answer: By simply making the deposit on January 1 instead of December 31, the money earned $11,950.63, or about $700 more than an ordinary annuity. Review the following table:

Beginning of Year	Amount of Deposit	Number of Years Earning Interest	Future Value (Value at the End of 5 Years)
1	$2,000	5	$2,000(1.06)^5 = $2,676.45$
2	$2,000	4	$2,000(1.06)^4 = $2,524.95$
3	$2,000	3	$2,000(1.06)^3 = $2,382.03$
4	$2,000	2	$2,000(1.06)^2 = $2,247.20$
5	$2,000	1	$2,000(1.06)^1 = $2,120.00$
			Total on December 31 of the fifth year $= $11,950.63$

To find the total using a geometric series, we note that the first term will now be earning interest for a full year, the first year, which is also the case with the last term.

This series is

$$\$2{,}000(1.06)^5 + \$2{,}000(1.06)^4 + \$2{,}000(1.06)^3 + \$2{,}000(1.06)^2 + \$2{,}000(1.06).$$

Note that this is the same as

$$1.06(\$2{,}000(1.06)^4 + \$2{,}000(1.06)^3 + \$2{,}000(1.06)^2 + \$2{,}000(1.06) + \$2{,}000).$$

That is, we have 1.06 times what we had before.
So, the sum is

$$1.06 \times \frac{\$2{,}000(1.06^5 - 1)}{1.06 - 1} = \$11{,}950.64.$$

Tell students that since we are using r as the common ratio, to avoid confusion, we will use x for interest rate; a is Pmt, the present value; and n is the number of payment periods. Then, by substituting,

$$FV_{ordinary\ annuity} = \frac{a(x^n - 1)}{x - 1} \quad \text{can be written as}$$

$$FV_{ordinary\ annuity} = Pmt\left[\frac{(1+r)^n - 1}{r}\right],$$

and

$$FV_{annuity\ due} = r \cdot \frac{a(x^n - 1)}{x - 1} \quad \text{can be written as}$$

$$FV_{annuity\ due} = Pmt\left[\frac{(1+r)^n - 1}{r}\right] \cdot (1+r).$$

Practice

1. At the beginning of each year, for 10 years, Martina deposits $1,000 of her bonus into an account that earns 7% annually:
   a. Identify this kind of investment.

    b. How much will she have at the end of 10 years, assuming no withdrawals?

    c. How much of that total is interest earned?

2. Harry begins contributing to IRAs starting at the end of his first year of work, when he is 22 years old. Each year for the next 40 years, he deposits $2,000 into an IRA that paid 6.5% annually:

    a. Identify this kind of investment.

    b. How much will he have at the end of the year that he turns 62, assuming no withdrawals?

    c. How much of that total is interest earned?

3. Connie needs $20,000 in 5 years to buy a car. To save this money, she decides to make equal payments each New Year's Day into an account paying 6% annually:

    a. Identify this kind of investment.

    b. How much will her payments need to be?

4. The company for which Joey works is downsizing and has offered him a buyout package. He can take either of the following:

    a. Lump sum of $ 80,000 now

    b. Payments of $10,000 each year for 10 years

    If he can invest either the lump sum or the annuity payments in an account that pays an annual rate of 9%, which choice should he make? Which account has the most money after 10 years?

5. Ashley is starting an annuity, into which she will make annual payments, to save money for her son's education. She thinks she can get an average of 6% annually on her money and wants to have enough money in the annuity to pay for her son to attend a school that costs $50,000 a year. If she starts contributing on the first of the year that he was born, what would be the least amount she would have to contribute yearly to the annuity so that it will be worth $200,000 the year her son turns 18?

6. Alison starts depositing $10,000 each year at the age of 25 into an ordinary annuity and continues until she is 35 and then does not touch the account until she is 55. Her twin brother starts depositing $10,000 each year at the age of 35 and continues until he is 55. If both of their investments earn 7%, who will have more in their account at age 55? If the interest rate is 4%, whose money has earned more ? If it's 10%, whose money has earned more?

7. If Lizzie saved $350 per month, at the beginning of the month, how much will she have at the end of 3 years, if the money could earn 6%?

8. What if Lizzie wanted to have $15,000 at the end of 5 years—what would she have to contribute monthly at the beginning of the month, and her investments could earn 5%?

Practice Answers

1. a. annuity due
   b. $14,783.60
   c. $4,783.60

2. a. ordinary annuity
   b. $351,263.83
   c. $271,263.83

3. a. annuity
   b. solving *FV* formula for *PV*, $3,347.10

4. After 10 years, the lump sum, if left untouched at 9%, would be worth $189,389, whereas an ordinary annuity would be worth $151,929, and an annuity due would be worth $165,602. Of course, without interest, after 10 years, $10,000 a year would give you $100,000 rather than $80,000. Before Joey makes his decision, he should consider his needs, how likely he is to spend a lump sum on wants, his current financial situation, and other investment options and get some trusted financial advice.

5. $6,105. Solving

$$FV_{annuity\ due} = Pmt \left[\frac{(1+r)^n - 1}{r} \right] \times (1+r)$$

for *Pmt*, we get

$$Pmt = FV_{annuity\ due} \times \frac{r}{[(1+r)^n - 1](1+r)},$$

so for Ashley:

$$Pmt = \$200,000 \times \frac{.06}{[(1.06)^{18} - 1](1.06)} = \$6,105.$$

This is the minimum yearly deposit needed to meet her goal.

6. To find out how much Alison earned, first use

$$FV_{ordinary\ annuity} = Pmt \left[\frac{(1+r)^n - 1}{r} \right]$$

to find out what she earned in the first 10 years when she was depositing into the account. Then use $FV = PV(1+r)^n$ where *PV is* $FV_{ordinary\ annuity}$, which was calculated just above.

   To find out what her twin brother earned, you need only the annuity formula. The results can also be found using a spreadsheet, the results of which are shown below. Note that Alison does better with the higher interest rates.

Interest Rate	Alison	Twin Brother
0.04	$263,069	$297,781
0.07	$534,653	$409,955
0.10	$1,072,190	$572,750

7. $14,593.69. This is shown with the formula for an annuity due and monthly compounding:

$$FV_{annuity\ due} = Pmt \left[\frac{(1+r)^n - 1}{r} \right] \times (1+r),$$

$$FV_{annuity\ due} = \$350 \left[\frac{\left(1 + \frac{.06}{12}\right)^{36} - 1}{\frac{.06}{12}} \right] \times \left(1 + \frac{.06}{12}\right) = \$14,593.69.$$

8. $385. If Lizzie wanted to have savings of $15,000 after 3 years and her money could earn 5%, we would use the annuity due formula, solved for *Pmt*.

$$FV_{annuity\ due} = Pmt \left[\frac{(1+r)^n - 1}{r} \right] \times (1+r).$$

$$\$15,000 = Pmt \left[\frac{\left(1 + \frac{.05}{12}\right)^{36} - 1}{\frac{.05}{12}} \right] \times \left(1 + \frac{.05}{12}\right) \rightarrow Pmt \approx \$385.$$

Credit Cards and Debt Management

Using Credit Seems Unreal

What's the first thing I tell someone who wants to get out of debt? Cut up all your credit cards!

—Debt Counselor

Using credit cards is now a permanent fixture in our money landscape. It is also a subject designed for math, with minimum payments and various interest rates. It is, in fact, a critical subject for young adults as they become savvy about money. There are a number of opportunities to weave money into math applications that address the National Council of Teachers of Mathematics (NCTM) standards.

NCTM STANDARDS APPLIED IN THIS CHAPTER

Content

- *Number and Operations.* Understand meanings of operations and how they relate to one another; compute fluently and make reasonable estimates.

(Continued)

(Continued)

- *Algebra.* Understand patterns, relations, and functions; represent and analyze mathematical situations and structures using algebraic symbols; use mathematical models to represent and understand quantitative relationships.

Process

- Problem Solving; Reasoning and Proof; Communication; Connections; Representation

BACKGROUND: BASICS OF CREDIT AND DEBIT CARDS

Why does using credit cards seem unreal? In past generations, we actually paid for things with real money, that is, money we had in the bank or money in our pocket.

With credit cards, we can buy things when we might not actually have the money. Yes, we hope we will have the money when the bill comes in, but by then, just maybe, we've already bought more things we hope we can pay for. Then, the amount we owe could start to escalate. While most people use common sense about what they can afford, some people can easily get into permanent debt all too quickly. Why? Because it's too easy to use a credit card to buy something.

With the newer-type debit cards, money is taken directly from your account when you make a purchase. Thus, it can be an effective way to keep your buying habits in check. If you don't actually have money in your account, you can't buy anything.

The problem with regular credit cards, however, is that once caught in the negative vortex of ever deepening debt, people find it difficult to get caught up. It's a race that's difficult not only to win but to even finish. It can seem like a never-ending treadmill.

Although we can preach about the dangers of credit card debt, we can also help young adults to understand these dangers by using math to illustrate the reality of debt.

TEACHING EXAMPLE 3.1

Calculating Minimum Monthly Payments

NCTM Content Standards

Numbers and Operations

Process Standards

Problem Solving; Connections

Money Applications

Students will

- Calculate the amount of minimum payment on a credit card
- Calculate the amount of monthly interest on a credit card
- Estimate roughly how long it would take to pay off a credit card balance if paid a fixed amount toward the balance each month

Discussion and Questions

Photo by Paul Westbrook.

Ask students what the "minimum" payment is required on a credit card balance. They will probably give several answers, but the minimum payment charged by most credit card companies is now 3% or 4%.

Ask students if the minimum payment is 4%, how much the monthly minimum payment is on an outstanding credit card balance of $3,000.

The answer is $120 since

$$\$3,000 \times .04 = \$120.$$

Now, ask students what interest rates credit card companies charge on the outstanding balance. It may surprise them to learn that although there are some low temporary rates used to entice customers, it is not unusual to pay over 20% on an annual basis! Also, credit card companies can increase the interest rate from a low initial rate to a much higher one if you're late on a payment. They may even charge a higher rate if you're late on a payment on another credit card, late with payments such as your electric bill or mortgage payment, or just because the company thinks you owe too much (as explained at www.pbs.org/wgbh/pages/frontline/shows/credit).

Ask students to calculate the interest on a credit card balance of $10,000 if the interest rate is 21.9% annually.

First, explain that credit card bills quote the annual and then the daily rate. Because the number of days in the months can vary, with a daily rate, they can calculate every little bit of interest. This daily rate is stated on the credit card bill, along with the annual rate.

Since we assume 365 days in a year, divide 21.9% by 365 to get the daily rate of 0.06%, as shown:

$$\frac{21.9\%}{365} = .06\% \text{ or, in decimal form, } \frac{0.219}{365} = .0006.$$

To translate this daily rate to a monthly rate, multiply by 30 or 31 (or 29 or 28 for February) for the days in the month. Assuming 30 days in a month, the monthly rate would be 1.8%:

$$.0006 \times 30 = 0.018 = 1.8\%.$$

Thus, the monthly finance charge, in our example, on a balance of $10,000 would be $180.

$$\$10,000 \times .018 = \$180.$$

Let's now compare this monthly finance charge to the minimum monthly payment the credit card requires.

If the minimum payment is 4%, then the minimum payment on $10,000 would be $400.

$$\$10,000 \times .04 = \$400.$$

The finance charge, in our example, is $180, whereas the minimum payment is $400. The difference is the money that is actually paid toward the principal. In this case, it is only $220 ($400 − $180 = $220).

Ask students how long it would take to pay off this $10,000 balance by paying $220 each month toward the principal. If we simply divide the 220 into 10,000, we get

$$\frac{\$10,000}{\$220 \text{ per month}} = 45.5 \text{ months} = 4 \text{ years.}$$

This is a very rough calculation because as the balance declines, the minimum payments and the finance charges also decline. The next teaching example shows how long it takes if rather than paying $220 per month toward the principal, we pay whatever the minimum payment is each month. Under those conditions, it takes about 22½ years to pay off the balance!

Practice

1. What is the minimum monthly payment if the minimum is 3% and the balance is $1,200?

2. What is the minimum monthly payment if the minimum is 4% and the balance is $2,500?

3. What is the daily interest rate if the annual rate is 18%?

4. What are the daily and monthly interest rates if the annual rate is 12.5%, assuming 30 days in the month?

Practice Answers

1. $36 ($1,200 times .03 equals $36).

2. $100 ($2,500 times .04 equals $100).

3. .0049% (.18 divided by 365 equals .00049, or .049%).

4. .034% daily, 1.02% monthly (.125 divided by 365 equals .00034, or .034%; .00034 times 30 equals .0102, or 1.02%).

Extension

Have the students think about how to perform the above minimum payment and interest calculations using a spreadsheet program.

Although there are several spreadsheet programs to use, we are using Microsoft Excel here. As with all spreadsheet programs, one must follow designated notation rules. For example, in Excel, one must always

- Refer to a cell by the letter of its column and the number of its row. So, B7 is the cell that is in column B and row 7.
- Enter an equals sign " = " before a formula.
- Enter a value as seen; for example, if one wants to enter "$2,000," it can be entered as shown. In some programs, one first enters the raw number of, say, 2000, then adds, through menus, commas and the dollar signs.

Furthermore, in Excel (like most programs), to enter an arithmetic operation, these symbols are used:

Addition	+
Subtraction	−
Multiplication	*
Division	/

With this beginning, let's create a simple spreadsheet of our credit card information. Let's find, during a sample month, how much interest will be charged and how much the minimum payment will be. We'll also find out how much the ending monthly balance will be given a certain monthly beginning balance.

First, let's set up a relatively simple spreadsheet:

Step 1: Enter Titles in a Spreadsheet as Follows

In A2, enter: **Calculating Interest and Minimum Payments**
In A4, enter: **SAMPLE MONTH**
In A7, enter: **Yearly Interest Rate:**
In A8, enter: **Monthly Interest Rate:**
In A10, enter: **Minimum Payment Percent:**
In A13, enter: **Balance at Beginning of Month**
In A14, enter: **Amount of Interest:**
In A15, enter: **Minimum Payment:**
In A16, enter: **Balance at End of Month:**

Your spreadsheet should now look like the following:

	A	B	C	D
1				
2	Calculating Interest and Minimum Payments			
3				
4	SAMPLE MONTH			
5				
6				
7	Yearly Interest Rate:			
8	Monthly Interest Rate:			
9				
10	Minimum Payment Percent:			
11				
12				
13	Balance at Beginning of Month:			
14	Amount of Interest:			
15	Minimum Payment:			
16	Balance at End of Month:			

Step 2: Enter Values and Formulas as Follows

In D7, enter the value of **21.9%**
In D8, enter the formula of $=$ **D7/365*30** (use upper- or lowercase letters)
In D10, enter the value of $=$ **3%**
In D13, enter the value of $=$ **2000**
In D14, enter the formula of $=$ **D13*D8**
In D15, enter the formula of $=$ **D13*D10**
In D16, enter the formula of $=$ **D13 $+$ D14-D15**

To format cells D13 through D16, highlight them and click on "$" in the toolbar.

Your spreadsheet should now provide the calculations you want:

	A	B	C	D
1				
2	Calculating Interest and Minimum Payments			
3				
4	SAMPLE MONTH			
5				
6				
7	Yearly Interest Rate:			21.90%
8	Monthly Interest Rate:			0.018
9				
10	Minimum Payment Percent:			3%
11				
12				
13	Balance at Beginning of Month:			$2,000
14	Amount of Interest:			$36
15	Minimum Payment:			$60
16	Balance at End of Month:			$1,976

Now replace the **Minimum Payment Percent:** from 3% to 4% and obtain a new **Minimum Payment:** of $80 and a new **Balance at End of Month:** of $1,956. The **Yearly Interest Rate:** can also be changed and the resulting **Balance at End of Month:** will be calculated.

TEACHING EXAMPLE 3.2

Credit Card Payoff: A Spreadsheet

NCTM Content Standards

Numbers and Operations; Algebra

Process Standards

Problem Solving; Reasoning and Proof; Communication; Connections; Representation

Money Applications

Students will

- Construct a spreadsheet
- Creatively solve the credit card problem using the power of the spreadsheet
- Determine the number of years to pay off credit card balances if only minimum payments are made

Discussion and Questions

Ask students how long it would actually take to pay off a $10,000 credit card balance if only the minimum payments were made each month. Further assume that the minimum payment would be 4% each month and also assume that no additional charges would be made to the credit card.

Have them record their conjectures, which will be compared later to the actual number of months, or years. Point out that unlike mortgages and car loans, credit card payments do not fit the annuity form of payments. Credit card payments use the declining balance method, with minimum payments declining as the balance declines. Thus, we cannot use the annuity formulas that we developed in Chapter 2.

After they record their guesses, tell them that since there doesn't seem to be an obvious formula to use, we'll turn to the use of a computer spreadsheet to solve this problem.

We will use these specific conditions:

1. A $10,000 credit card balance

2. An annual interest rate of 21.9% on the outstanding balance

3. A minimum payment of 4% of the outstanding balance

4. If the balance is $25 or less, full payment must be made

5. The maximum payment schedule is 35 years

6. A 30-day month is assumed for all months

In our spreadsheet, we will be able to actually calculate each month's beginning balance, the interest we have to pay, our minimum payment, and the ending balance. We can construct the spreadsheet to do this for each month until we find our answer.

Furthermore, we will set up the spreadsheet to allow for the calculation for differing balances, interest rates, and minimum payments. Thus, we will have a ready-made method to find any solution.

Although there are a number of spreadsheet programs, we'll use the Excel spreadsheet by Microsoft in our example. There are three parts to the construction of the spreadsheet.

Part 1: Enter Basic Information Into the Spreadsheet

To begin constructing our spreadsheet, we enter some basic information, so our spreadsheet will look like the following:

```
     A        B        C        D        E        F        G        H
1  How many years to pay off credit card balance, if paying just minimum?
2
3  Balance:                     $10,000
4
5  Annual Interest Rate:        21.90%
6
7  Minimum Payment Percent:     4.00%
8
9  Answer:       22.5 Years
10
11 Notes: 1) If balance is $25 or less, full payment must be made.
12        2) Maximum payment schedule is 35 years.
```

The steps to achieve the above results are as follows:

- Begin at cell number A1 and enter as text: **How many years to pay off credit card balance, if paying just minimum?**
- In A3, enter as text: **Balance:**
- In D3, enter **10000** as an initial value. Note that no dollar sign or comma is entered. To show a dollar sign and comma for thousands, first click on Format in the menu options and then click on Cells. Finally, choose "currency" from the dialog menu. Also, since we are rounding to the nearest whole dollar, make sure the "decimal places" section of the dialog box shows "0."
- In A5, enter as text: **Annual Interest Rate:**
- In D5, enter **21.9%**. If it is entered with a percent sign, the cell automatically converts to the decimal equivalent.
- In A7, enter as text: **Minimum Payment Percentage:**
- In D7, enter **4.00%**
- In A9, enter as text: **Answer:**
- In D9, enter as text: **Years**

- In A11, enter dashes to separate these initial data from any notes or comments that will be added below.
- In A12 and A13, enter two notes: **(1) If balance is $25 or less, full payment must be made.**, and **(2) Maximum payment schedule is 35 years.** (The first note follows many credit card companies' requirement that if the balance is small, it must be paid off that month. The second note pertains to a limit we want for this exercise, so it doesn't go on forever.)
- In C15, enter: **Months**
- In D15, enter the number **1** (this is the first of many months that our spreadsheet will cover).
- In A17 through A20, enter the following four titles, respectively: **Balance Beginning of Month:**, **Monthly Interest:**, **Monthly Minimum Payment:**, and **Balance End of Month:**.

	A	B	C	D
15			Months	1
16				
17	Balance Beginning of Month:			$10,000
18	Monthly Interest:			180
19	Monthly Minimum Payment:			400
20	Balance End of Month:			$9,780

Part 2: Enter Basic Formulas as Follows

Add the following, as bulleted below, to the spreadsheet so that it will look like the spreadsheet above.

Note that all values are rounded to the nearest whole number. The spreadsheet formulas are then as follows:

- In D17, enter = **D3,** the cell position of the starting balance, which in our example is $10,000.
- In D18, enter = **($D$5/365)*30)*D17,** the formula to calculate the monthly interest. Note that $D$5 indicates that the amount in D5, the annual interest rate, is a constant; that $D$5/365 gives the daily interest rate; and that ($D$5/365)*30 gives the monthly rate based on a 30-day month. Also note that constants are referenced with a $ before the letter and number of the cell, as shown above, as in $D$3, so that when we copy them across the rows or columns, they will remain constant.
- In D19, enter = **D17*$D$7,** the formula to calculate the monthly minimum payment. We want to always use the beginning-of-the-month balance (D17 in this case) but always use our minimum payment percent, D7. It is a constant, so it is written as $D$7.
- In D20, enter = **IF(D17 + D18 − D19 > = 25, D17 + D18 − D19,0).** Use the Format function in the Menu to format for currency and no decimals. This cell calculates what our balance will be after we add the monthly interest and subtract the monthly minimum payment. It will also enter a zero if the balance falls below 25.

Part 3: Use the Copy Function to Solve the Problem

Tell the students that the last part of constructing our spreadsheet requires that we enter some more information, use the Copy function (to spread out the months), and then devise a creative solution to determine when the balance is zero. It's at that point that we'll find our answer. Thus, next:

- In E15, enter = **D15 + 1.** This formula adds "1" to each year.
- In E17, enter = **D20,** the result of the previous month, which is the end-of-month balance.
- In E18 through E20, copy D18 through D20. This is accomplished by using the Copy and Paste function of Excel. First, highlight the cells that are to be copied, D18 through D20, and then right-click with the mouse and select **copy.** Then move the cursor, with the mouse, over the beginning of the cells where the cells are to be copied, E18, and then right-click with the mouse and select **paste.**

	A	B	C	D	E	F	G	H
15			Months	1	2	3	4	5 ···
16								
17	Balance Beginning of Month:			$10,000	$9,780	$9,565	$9,354	$9,149
18	Monthly Interest:			180	176	172	168	165
19	Monthly Minimum Payment:			400	391	383	374	366
20	Balance End of Month:			$9,780	$9,565	$9,354	$9,149	$8,947

- Now the spreadsheet is set up to spread out as far to the right as the worksheet will allow. Do this by copying E15 through E20 to F15 through IV20. Since the spreadsheet goes only this far, we'll have to see if that is far enough.

Your spreadsheet should now look like this:

	A	B	C	D	E	F	G	H
15			Months	1	2	3	4	5 ···
16								
17	Balance Beginning of Month:			$10,000	$9,780	$9,565	$9,354	$9,149
18	Monthly Interest:			180	176	172	168	165
19	Monthly Minimum Payment:			400	391	383	374	366
20	Balance End of Month:			$9,780	$9,565	$9,354	$9,149	$8,947
30			Months	254	255	256	257	258
31								
32	Balance Beginning of Month:			$36	$35	$34	$34	$33
33	Monthly Interest:			1	1	1	1	1
34	Monthly Minimum Payment:			1	1	1	1	1
35	Balance End of Month:			$35	$34	$34	$33	$32

This spreadsheet continues through cells IV15–IV20, where it ends (no, spreadsheets don't extend forever).

However, when we examine the values at that point, given our example, we find that we still have a balance in IV20 of $36, which means that we need to extend the information even further.

We do this by starting another section of rows just below the first section. We start the second section with the row of cells beginning as row 30, as shown above.

To accomplish these entries:

- Copy the titles from A15 to C20 to A30 through C35.
- In D30, enter **= IV15 + 1,** the formula to add "1" to the last year in IV15.
- In E30, enter: **= D30 + 1.** Then copy the cell E30 to the section of F30 through to IV30. This extends the number of months from D30 onward.
- In D32, enter **= IV20,** the formula to take the ending balance from IV20.
- In D33 through D35, copy D18 through D20, the same formulas as in a normal month.
- In E32, enter **= D35**, then copy D33 through D35 to E33 through E35. This will now show the balance for this 254th month of $35.

Now we can extend the worksheet all the way to the right by using the Copy function (one of the powerful but simple functions of spreadsheets).

- Copy E32 through E35 to F32 through IV35.

We now have two elongated sections that calculate the end-of-year balances for 506 months since each section is 253 cells long. This is equivalent to 42 years (506 divided by 12 equals 42.16 years, rounded to 42 years), which is sufficient for our spreadsheet purpose since we limited it to 35 years.

Now comes the creative part:

- How can we have Excel identify the month when the balance will be zero?

	A	B	C	D	E	F	G	H
13								
14								
15			Months	1	2	3	4	5
16								
17	Balance Beginning of Month:			$10,000	$9,780	$9,565	$9,354	$9,149
18	Monthly Interest:			180	176	172	168	165
19	Monthly Minimum Payment:			400	391	383	374	366
20	Balance End of Month:			$9,780	$9,565	$9,354	$9,149	$8,947
21								
22				1	1	1	1	1
23								
24	Number of Month:		0	0	0	0	0	0
25								
26								
27								
28								
29								
30			Months	254	255	256	257	258
31								
32	Balance Beginning of Month:			$36	$35	$34	$34	$33
33	Monthly Interest:			1	1	1	1	1
34	Monthly Minimum Payment:			1	1	1	1	1
35	Balance End of Month:			$35	$34	$34	$33	$32
36								
37				1	1	1	1	1
38								
39	Number of Month:		270	0	0	0	0	0

This will give us our spreadsheet answer and allow us to report this information in cell B9.

There are a number of creative ways to approach this. One way is to construct two rows for each section that will identify, first, the specific cell where the balance is 0 (zero) and, second, what month this occurs. To do this, observe what the spreadsheet will look like (shown above) with the instructions that follow.

We will be using the IF statement, which is one of the most powerful logical spreadsheet functions:

In D22, enter the following logic formula: **= IF(OR(D17 = 0,D20> = 25),1,0).** This formula says that if the number in D17 is 0 or if the number in D20 is greater than or equal to 25, then 1 is placed in cell D22. If not, then the value of 0 is placed in the cell. This allows for only that one month, when a zero is produced, to be identified, and not any subsequent month. So, it will identify just the month that we want.

Generally, an IF statement has three elements: (1) a statement or condition (if the condition is compound, as in our example, then it is in parentheses), (2) a specific value if true, and (3) if not true, another specific value. Commas separate these three elements, and the whole statement has parentheses around it. An OR statement gives a disjunctive condition. AND conditions give a conjunctive condition.

- Now copy D22 to cells E22 to IV22. This copies the formula all across the row.

To complete this identification process, in cell D24, create an IF statement to produce the number of the month when the balance is first zero. To accomplish this:

- In D24, enter = **IF(D22 = 0,D15,0).** This will put in the cell the actual number of months we are trying to isolate.
- Then, copy D24 to cells E24 to IV24.
- In A24 enter the text: **Number of Month:**
- In C24, enter = **SUM(D24:IV24).** This sums the entire row. Since there are zeros in every cell in the row except for the month in which the balance is entirely paid off or less than or equal to $25, we get that month.

Since we have two sections, repeat the instructions above (rows 22 and 24) for rows 37 and 39.

Your spreadsheet should now give the answer, in months, in either cell C24 or C39.

Our final step will simply bring the answer up to B9:

- In B9, enter: = **IF((C24 + C39)/12>35,35,(C24 + C39)/12).** Keep in mind that C24 sums everything in row 24 from C24 across, and thanks to the Copy function, C39 sums everything in row 39 from C39 across. So C24 + C39 sums those two rows, which gives the number of months required to pay off the balance. Dividing by 12 gives the number of years to pay off the balance. The number of years cannot exceed 35, so if we get a result larger than 35, then "35" is placed in cell B9, and if not, then the actual number of years, (C24 + C39)/12, is placed in the cell.

This now completes our spreadsheet with the answer of how long it would take to pay off a credit card balance of $10,000 if only the minimum payments are made and no new charges are applied to that card:

Answer: 22.5 years!

The upper part of the spreadsheet should now look like the following:

	A	B	C	D	E	F	G
1	How many years to pay off credit card balance, if paying just minimum?						
2							
3	Balance:			$10,000			
4							
5	Annual Interest Rate:			21.90%			
6							
7	Minimum Payment Percentage:			4.00%			
8							
9	Answer:		22.5 Years				
10							

(Comment: Good grief! The moral of this story is this: *Do not* use a credit card unless you will have the money to pay the credit card balance off within a short period of time.)

You can now enter any balance, any annual interest rate, or any minimum payment percentage to calculate the time required to completely pay that debt.

Practice

1. Calculate the number of years to pay off a $10,000 balance, with 10% annual interest, and a minimum payment of 2%.

2. Calculate the number of years to pay off a $20,000 balance, with 15% annual interest, and a minimum payment of 5%.

3. Calculate the number of years to pay off a $30,000 balance, with 21.9% annual interest, and a minimum payment of 4%.

Practice Answers

1. 35 years.

2. 14.6 years.

3. 26.6 years.

Extensions

1. Offer students a challenge to simplify the above spreadsheet by having the results appear only in rows 24 and 39, rather than using the two row solutions for each set, that of rows 22–24 and rows 37–39.

2. Have students derive recursive and explicit formulas for finding the remaining balance at the end of any month, if just the minimum payment is made. Challenge them to use one of those formulas to find the time it will take to pay off the balance. They can first develop an algorithm for the balance at the end of any month. An algorithm that leads to the recursive formula is as follows: Find the difference between the minimum payment and the interest payment and then subtract that from the old balance to find the new balance. Using the givens in this teaching example, and letting the balance at the end of month m be symbolized as B_m and

the balance at the end of the previous month be B_{m-1}, our algorithm can be represented, using the 4% minimum balance payment and the 1.8% daily interest, by the following equation: $B_m = B_{m-1} - (0.04B_{m-1} - 0.018B_{m-1})$. Simplifying, we have $B_m = 0.088B_{m-1}$. Recognizing the geometric nature of the progression, this relationship can be explicitly expressed as $B_m = 0.088^m(\$10,000)$. Using the formula to solve for the month in which the balance is 0 is tricky since there is no solution to $0 = 0.088^m(\$10,000)$, but students could solve by using a small balance such as $25, the amount at which the balance must be paid off anyway.

Investments

The Basics and More

Only buy something that you'd be perfectly happy to hold if the market shut down for 10 years.

—Warren Buffett

An important aspect of handling your money involves understanding investments. Not only is this an essential topic for everyday living, thereby becoming a real situation for students, but it also offers a number of useful opportunities for weaving money into math discussions while applying the National Council of Teachers of Mathematics (NCTM) standards. (The terms used in this chapter can be found in the Money Glossary, starting on page 145.)

NCTM STANDARDS APPLIED IN THIS CHAPTER

Content

- *Number and Operations.* Understand numbers, ways of representing numbers; understand meanings of operations and how they relate to one another; compute fluently and make reasonable estimates.
- *Algebra.* Understand patterns, relations, and functions; represent and analyze mathematical situations and structures using algebraic symbols; use mathematical models to represent and understand quantitative relationships.

(Continued)

(Continued)

- *Data Analysis and Probability.* Select and use appropriate statistical methods to analyze data.

Process

- Problem Solving; Reasoning and Proof; Communication; Connections; Representation

BACKGROUND: BASICS OF INVESTMENTS

What Is an Investment?

An investment is simply the use of money for the purpose of making more money.

Keeping your money in the pocket of your jeans is not an investment since the money in your pocket will grow only if you put more money into your pocket. That money will never grow on its own. However, if your money earns compound interest in "safe investments" such as savings accounts, CDs, or money market accounts, then your money will definitely earn more money. And if money is put into stocks, bonds, or mutual funds, then your money has the potential of earning even more money.

Why Study Investments?

We study investments because we want know how to make our money grow so that we can afford to buy a house (itself a great investment), send our children to college, see the world, explore our interests, and retire in comfort. The goal of investing is thus financial security, and the best way to reach that goal is to start young. In giving many seminars over the years, people often say the following: I wish I understood investments early in my life—and—why don't they teach this in school?

Let's Start With Stocks

Stocks are a perfectly good place to start. Why? Because over the years, they have been the best investment, outside of one's house. Since 1926, the average stock market return has been about 12%. That means that each year, on average, the market has been up 12%. Of course, not every year—some years it has been above that, such as the 5 years from 1995 to 1999. Some years it has been below that, such as the 3 years after 1999.

But on average, this 12% return beats the other basic investments: bonds, money market accounts, and CDs. Since 1926, the average return for bonds has been about 6%, and money market accounts and CDs, about 4%. So, stocks have been up twice as much as bonds and three times as much as money market accounts and CDs.

Stocks Are Often Called "Equity"

Why? Because they represent ownership in companies. Since our economy has done quite well over the years, company stock values, which tend to follow the economy in general, have done well. Thus, stocks are an important investment a person should be familiar with. Actually, stocks are an ideal subject to study math. Although stocks have returned 12% each year over the long term, they are volatile. That is, they don't always return 12%. In the world of investments, we call this volatility risk. Furthermore, we measure this volatility with the statistical measure of standard deviation. Precisely, we use one standard deviation for risk, which would represent the volatility over about 68% of the time.

You've heard of *risk* and *return* on investments. Well, risk is standard deviation, and return is just that, the 1-year average return or, as we say in math, the mean. We can also get fancy by also using correlations and finding the average standard deviation of a combined portfolio, which we will do later in the chapter. These are mathematical tools that teach or reinforce useful mathematical formulas and equations that are also used in other mathematical areas. Furthermore, it is our experience that students prefer practical and useful problems. None could be more so than investments and other aspects of personal finance.

To give you more precise investment numbers, here are the average one-year returns and their standard deviations (rounded to the nearest percent):

	Average 1-Year Return	*Standard Deviation or Risk*
Stock Market (S&P 500)[a]	12%	20%
Bonds	6%	9%
Money Market Accounts and CDs	4%	3%

a. See the Money Glossary—it's the average price of the largest 500 companies.

This recalls the following phrase: no risk, no reward.

But What About Bonds?

Bonds are an important part of investments. So, how do they work and how are they different from stocks?

Bonds Pay Interest on a Regular Basis, Usually Twice a Year

This interest is primarily why people buy bonds. It usually is the highest interest an investor can find. Furthermore, the longer the maturity of the bond, the higher the interest rate. When a bond is offered, it can be for as short as 3 months (a 3-month Treasury bill) or as long as 30 or 50 years for a corporate bond. Typically, a bond is for 5 to 15 years.

So, interest payments are key. Although stocks can pay dividends (usually quarterly), the dividend rate is quite low, about 1% of the stock price. Thus, you buy bonds for interest, but you buy stocks for growth.

Corporations are not the only issuers of bonds. The U.S. Treasury issues T-bills (Treasury bills) of 1 year or less, T-notes of 2 to 10 years, and T-bonds for 20 or 30 years. And municipalities and states also issue bonds. These are for public works projects that require large upfront money with the municipality able to repay the loan back over many years. For the investor, they typically are free of income tax on both the federal and state levels (for state tax exclusion, they have to be issued by the state you reside in).

Bonds, which are called fixed-income securities, have a different characteristic than stocks. *The market value of bonds moves in the opposite direction from the movement of interest rates.* If interest rates are moving up, the value of bonds moves down. Likewise, if interest rates move down, then the value of bonds moves up. Yes, an inverse relationship. If, however, an investor holds the bond to maturity, then the bond pays its full par or face value.

The percent of bond value that is gained or lost can be calculated by *duration.* It's not the length of maturity per se; it is a weighted present value of all payments. For instance, the maturity of a 5-year bond has a duration of about 3%. This means that if interest rates moved 1 percentage point upward, the value of bonds would move 3% downward. If interest rates move a full 2 percentage points upward, the value of bonds would move 6% downward.

Ten-year bonds have a duration of about 7%, 15-year bonds have a duration of about 10%, and 20-year bonds have a duration of about 12%. That is, for instance, if 10-year interest rates moved down one full percentage point, the value of 10-year bonds would increase by approximately 7%.

What Are Money Market Accounts?

Money market accounts or funds are short-term interest investments at banks and mutual funds. They usually pay less than bonds, but there are times, such as in October 2005, when bonds are only a percentage point higher. Usually, there is a bigger difference, often 2% to 4% higher.

The Key to Money Market Accounts Is That They Don't Lose Any Value

This is why people appropriately think of them as safe investments, even though they pay a lower amount of interest.

What Are CDs, or Certificates of Deposit?

They are offered by banks as a fixed-income investment from as short as 3 months to as long as 5 years. During that time, the interest is fixed, as designated when it was offered. Like bonds, the interest is fixed, or constant, once it is offered. Thus, an investor of a CD simply collects the designated interest, usually monthly, biannually, or annually.

A "Portfolio" Is a Mix of Stocks, Bonds, Money Market Accounts, and Sometimes CDs

People don't invest in just one type of investment. Why not? Because of prudence. If people invested in only stocks, they would have a good deal of volatility in their overall portfolio. Usually too much to feel comfortable. Why not, then, just bonds, money market accounts, or CDs? Because a person could potentially lose the opportunity to make more money. Or, to put it positively, a person would have a chance to make more money if he or she is invested in stocks. After all, over an extended period of time, stocks have earned an average of 12% versus 6% for bonds and 4% for money market accounts and CDs.

What to Do?

Invest in a combination, or what is called diversification. A typical "growth" portfolio has about 65% in stocks, 35% in bonds and CDs, and 5% in money market accounts. A "conservative" portfolio has about 35% in stocks, 60% in bonds and CDs, and 5% in money market accounts. The higher percent in stocks should bring a higher return, but only long term, usually measured as 10 years or more. Because of the volatility of stocks, short-term results can obviously vary considerably.

And that's investments in a nutshell.

TEACHING EXAMPLE 4.1

Stock Prices and Percents

NCTM Content Standards

Numbers and Operations

Process Standards

Problem Solving; Reasoning and Proof; Communication; Connections

Money Applications

Students will

- Calculate cost of purchasing stock
- Calculate percent increase/decrease
- Calculate P/E ratio

Discussion and Questions

SOURCE: Used with permission from McDonald's Corporation.

Engage students by asking them when they were last at McDonald's, and then ask the following questions about this fast-food giant:

1. How many McDonald's restaurants are there?

   Answer: McDonald's has more than 30,000 restaurants in more than 119 countries (see www.mcdonalds.com).

2. How many people eat at McDonald's every day?

   Answer: They serve about 50 million people each day.

3. When did McDonald's begin and how?

   Answer: In 1954, Ray Kroc mortgaged his home and invested his entire life savings to be the exclusive distributor of a milkshake maker called the Multimixer. When he heard that a hamburger stand called McDonald's was using eight of his mixers at a time, he convinced the owners of the stand, the McDonald brothers, to open more restaurants so that he could sell them his Multimixers. Ray ended up buying the McDonald's name and running those restaurants, and with the money from those investments, he opened more and more and more restaurants.

4. When did McDonald's first sell stock to the public, and why do companies offer stock this way?

   Answer: In 1965, McDonald's went public with the company's first offering on the stock exchange. A hundred shares of stock costing a total of $2,250 that day would have multiplied into 74,360 shares today, worth over $2.5 million on January 1, 2006. In 1985, McDonald's was added to the 30-company Dow Jones Industrial Average (the average price of 30 selected stocks, which is meant to be representative of our economy as a whole).

Companies sell stock to the public in order to raise money that allows them to operate, innovate, and expand.

Ask students the following questions based on the information above:

How much money did that $2,250 investment earn over the 38 years from 1965 through 2005?

Answer: $2,500,000 − $2,250 = $2,497,750

What percent increase is this of the original $2,250?

Answer: Huge! 111,000%. The starting value was $2,250, and the ending value was $2,500,000, so the difference is $2,497,750.

$$\text{Percent of increase is} = \frac{\text{Difference}}{\text{Starting Value}} \times 100\%$$

$$\text{Percent of increase is} = \frac{\$2,497,750}{\$2,250} \times 100\% = 1,110 \times 100\% = 111,000\%.$$

Practice

Have students work individually or as a group to solve the problems in the set. The problems refer to the information below, found at Yahoo! Finance (http://finance.yahoo.com). Please note that brokerage fees are not considered in these problems, but please point out to students that stockbrokers do charge fees for buying and selling stock.

This information is for McDonald's, ticker symbol: MCD, as of July 28, 2006:

MCDONALDS CP (NYSE: MCD)

Last Trade:	**34.81**	Day's Range:	34.72–34.94
Trade Time:	Jul 28	52wk Range:	30.10–36.75
Change:	↑0.08 (0.23%)	Volume:	5,201,100
Prev Close:	34.73	Avg Vol (3m):	5,664,530
Open:	34.80		
Bid:	N/A	Market Cap:	43.38B
Ask:	N/A	P/E (ttm):	15.69
1y Target Est:	40.75	EPS (ttm):	2.22
		Div Yield (ttm):	0.67 (1.90%)

1. How much would you have paid if you bought 100 shares of MCD at the last trade indicated on July 28?

2. If you bought your 100 shares at the lowest price in the last 52 weeks, how much would your investment have appreciated by the last trade indicated on July 28? State as a dollar amount and as a percent of increase.

3. If you bought 1,000 shares at the lowest price during the last 52 weeks, how much would your investment have appreciated by the last trade indicated on July 28? State as a dollar amount and as a percent of increase.

4. If you bought 3,000 shares at the lowest price in the last 52 weeks, how much would your investment have appreciated by the last trade indicated on July 28? State as a dollar amount and as a percent of increase.

5. Why doesn't the amount of stock purchased affect the percent of increase?

6. Recently, MCD declared a dividend of $.67/share. How many shares would you have had to own on that date, using the last trade July 28 price, in order to earn enough in dividends to buy one more share that day?

7. How many shares could you buy if you reinvested dividends from 1,000 shares at the last price?

8. Remember that in 1965, McDonald's went public with the company's first offering on the stock exchange. A hundred shares of stock costing $2,250 that day would have multiplied into 74,360 shares, worth $1.8 million on December 31, 2003. So,
   a. What was the price per share at the time of the initial public offering (IPO)?
   b. What was the price per share on December 31, 2003?

9. The P/E ratio is the price of the stock divided by the earnings per share of the company. The table gives this as 15.69. How can you calculate it from other information in the table? (The P/E ratio is considered one of the most important ratios in analyzing the stock of a company. It takes the current price of the stock divided by the earning per share of the stock. The average P/E ratio of all stocks, as measured by Standard & Poor's 500, as of January 1, 2006, was about 18.)

Practice Answers

1. $3,481 ($34.81 times 100 equals $3,481).

2. $471 and 15.6% ($30.10 times 100 equals $3,010; $34.81 times 100 equals $3,481; difference is $471; $471 divided by $3,010 equals .156 or 15.6%).

3. $4,710 and 15.6% (multiply by 1,000 instead of 100).

4. $14,130 and 15.6% (multiply by 3,000 instead of 100).

5. Because percent just gives you the change per 100 and not the dollar value.

6. Fifty-two shares ($34.81 divided by $0.67 equals 51.96 shares; rounding up equals 52).

7. Nineteen shares (1,000 times $0.67 equals $670; $670 divided by $34.81 equals 19.25 or 19 full shares).

8. a. $22.50.
   b. $24.20 ($1,800,000 divided by $74,360 equals $24.20).

9. Not precisely, but very close, because the P/E ratio of 15.69 in the table uses the share price as of December 31, 2005, which is not given. However, using the current price of $34.81, the P/E ratio is 15.68, which is quite close ($34.81 divided by 2.22, the earnings per share, equals 15.68).

Extension

Have students choose a specific company to research and report on to the class. Their report should contain information about the products or services that the company offers and basic information about its stock. In particular, their report should include the following data:

- Ticker symbol for the company
- High and low price for the past 52 weeks
- Number of shares traded the day before
- Closing price (which is sometimes listed as the last trading price)
- Annual dividend, if any
- Yield, if a dividend is paid
- P/E ratio

In addition, have the students answer the questions given in the preceding Practice section with respect to their stock.

TEACHING EXAMPLE 4.2

Analyzing Graphs of Stock Prices

NCTM Content Standards

Numbers and Operations; Algebra

Process Standards

Problem Solving; Reasoning and Proof; Communication; Connections; Representation

Money Applications

Students will

- Use graphs to determine trends in stock prices
- Compare graphs of different companies to determine differences and similarities in stock price trends
- Apply information from graphs to solve problems

Discussion and Questions

Engage students by having them imagine that they have been given $10,000 to invest in stocks. Ask them how they would decide which stocks to buy.

Tell students that one way that people decide which stocks to buy is by analyzing graphs that illustrate stock activity because they help us to see trends in stock prices as well as high and low prices over time. (This is called technical analysis because it uses just the movement of stock prices. The other way is to examine how well a business sector is doing and how well a specific company within that sector is doing versus their competition. This is called fundamental analysis.)

Explain that these graphs are unlike the graphs most often used in algebra because in algebra, we usually deal with relationships that can be represented by equations with independent and dependent variables. Unfortunately, there are no functional rules that define these graphs. If there were, the future prices of stock could be accurately predicted. Wouldn't that be sweet?

The graphs of stock activity show the movement of prices over time. They track the ups and downs of prices and can quite easily show the direction of price movements. Trends are then apparent, and predictions can be made based on those trends but without any guarantees.

Show students the following graph of McDonald's stock movements at a point in 2005:

Mcdonalds corp as of 22–jul–2005

Tell students that the upper part of the diagram is a line graph showing the price, in dollars, of one share of McDonald's stock over the time period. This part shows a full year's stock price performance, from July 23, 2004, through July 22, 2005. Point out that the price went from just over $27 (by eyeballing it) to a high of just over $34 in early March 2005 and settled around $31 on July 22, 2005.

Now explain that the lower part shows a bar graph of the volume of stock, in millions, that was traded on each day. That's a lot of shares traded, although a number of the trades were probably block trades with hundreds, or thousands, of shares traded as a single order. These large trades are often done by institutions or pension funds that hold large numbers of many stocks.

Point out that the volume of stock traded can show spikes of highs or lows. For instance, although the volume of McDonald's shows a general level of volume of from 4 to 5 million shares (by eyeballing it), there were some spikes of 10 to 15 million shares. There were also some trading days where the volume appears to be only 2 to 3 million.

Ask your students the following questions based on the upper graph:

1. How much did McDonald's stock increase in value from the beginning of September 2004 and New Year's Day of 2005?

   Answer: About $5. (Price on January 1 − Price on September 1 = $32 − $27)

2. Suppose that you invested as much as possible of your $1,000 in McDonald's stock on January 1, 2005:
   a. How many shares could you have purchased?
   b. What would those shares be worth on July 4, 2005?

   Answers:
   a. 31 shares
   b. $1,023 (31 × $33 = $1,023)

Ask your students the following questions based on the lower graph:

3. Can you see a relationship between when the volume spiked and the movement in prices?

   Answer: Spikes in volume (lower graph) correspond to dramatic price changes upward or downward (upper graph).

4. What kind of news do you think might make people want to buy McDonald's?

   Answer: Good profit report, more people eating burgers, Ronald McDonald House good publicity, etc.

5. What kind of news might make them want to sell it?

   Answer: Bad profit report, outbreak of mad-cow disease, Ronald McDonald arrested for DUI, and so on.

6. Identify two points at which the volume spiked upward. Describe the action of the price of the stock at that time.

   Answer: Mid-October and mid-July volume spiked and price went up sharply. Also, in early June, there were a couple of spikes, and the price dropped sharply.

NOTE: Point out to students that although specific news can drive a stock up or down, realize that a stock could move because of unseen forces at work. For instance, institutions or large pension funds may make a decision about buying or selling a stock because their internal models indicated to do so. These models are mathematically complex and can include internal portfolio interworkings with other investments.

Practice

Show students the following graph of two stocks, McDonald's and Wendy's, and then ask students the questions that follow.

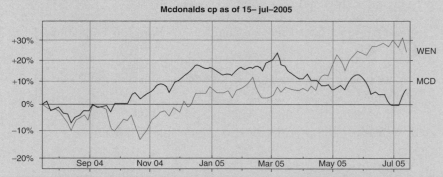

Mcdonalds cp as of 15– jul–2005

SOURCE: Reproduced with permission of Yahoo! Inc. © 2006 by Yahoo! Inc. YAHOO! and the YAHOO! logo are trademarks of Yahoo! Inc.

At the open of trading on July 16, 2004, McDonald's (MCD) was worth $27.80/share, and Wendy's (WEN) was worth $36.50/share.

1. Why is the *y*-intercept the same for the Wendy's and McDonald's graphs?

2. Describe the performance of both stocks in mid-August 2004.

3. When was the McDonald's stock worth more than $27.80/share?

4. If you had wanted to sell after McDonald's exceeded $33/share, when would you have sold?

5. Which stock performed better overall during the year shown? Explain.

6. What is the significance of points at which the two graphs intersect? Use one of those points to illustrate your answer.

7. Compare the activity of both stocks between March 1, 2005, and May 1, 2005.

8. Suppose that you had purchased 100 shares of McDonald's at the opening price on July 16, 2004. Approximately how much would those 100 shares be worth on November 1, 2004?

9. When would those 100 McDonald's shares be worth the most? The least?

10. Suppose you had also bought 100 shares of Wendy's stock at the opening price on July 16, 2004, and that you sold all 200 shares on July 16, 2005. Which stock would have made a greater profit? Explain.

Practice Answers

1. Because the graph shows the percent increases or decreases. It doesn't show the actual stock prices, only the changes in percents.

2. They both decreased, with Wendy's decreasing about 10% and McDonald's about 8%.

3. Whenever it was above the 0% line. In this case, McDonald's stock was above the line about mid-September 2004. It again fell back to the 0% line around July 5, 2005.

4. Around March 1, 2005. (First find the percent increase [the difference of $33 subtracted from $27.80 equals $5.20], then divide by the starting price of $27.80, which equals 0.187, or 18.7%. Then, find on the graph where the price was about 18.7% higher, which was about March 1, 2005.)

5. Wendy's. Although McDonald's percent exceeded Wendy's for most of the period, Wendy's moved ahead in late April and stayed ahead.

6. Their stock increase was equal for the year at that point. There was only one point where this happened.

7. Their price increases were going in the opposite direction.

8. About $2,446 (first, multiply 100 by $27.80, which equals $2,780. Then, estimate the percent increase or decrease on November 1, which was about −12%. Find the dollar amount of −12% by multiplying $2,780 by −0.12, which equals −$333.60. Finally, subtract $333.60 from $2,780, equaling $2,446).

9. The most just after March 5, 2005, the least around mid-October, 2004.

10. Wendy's. Wendy's percent increase was higher on that date.

Extension

1. Have students create a graph with a spreadsheet program of a particular stock. You can also have the students create a combination graph of two stocks, as shown above with McDonald's and Wendy's. Graphing the results with a spreadsheet can provide a useful practice in using the computer to plot data. Have the students observe the closing price of a particular stock for each day for 1 or 2 weeks. This also gives the student experience in capturing data. Then have the student graph the data with a spreadsheet program. Although there are several spreadsheet programs, Excel is used here because it is common. This exercise can also be done by hand plotting if computers are either not available or convenient.

    Here's an example:

    Assume daily information for 10 days in October. Create a graph in Excel or another spreadsheet program as shown:

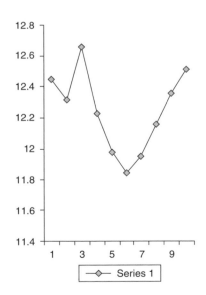

October	
1	12.45
2	12.32
3	12.66
4	12.23
5	11.98
6	11.84
7	11.95
8	12.16
9	12.36
10	12.51

2. Have students search archives of newspapers (or other media) at the time that a spike occurred in the volume of McDonald's or Wendy's stock price for an event that may have caused that spike.

TEACHING EXAMPLE 4.3

*Statistics of Stock I: Measures of Center,
Standard Deviation, Normal Distribution*

NCTM Content Standards

Numbers and Operations; Algebra; Data Analysis; Probability

Process Standards

Problem Solving; Reasoning and Proof; Communication; Connections;
Representation

Money Applications

Students will

- Calculate measures of center and standard deviation
- Analyze normal distributions and the bell-shaped curve

Part A: Mean, Median, and Mode

Discussion and Questions

Tell students that the measures of central tendency that they have learned can
help them understand stock prices so that they can make wise decisions on which
stocks to buy.

In the way of review, ask students to define mean, median, and mode. They
should tell you the following:

1. The *mean* is the average of a set of numbers. Symbolically,

$$\text{Mean} \ \ \text{or} \ \ \bar{x} = \frac{\text{sum of the numbers}}{\text{number of data points}} = \frac{x_1 + x_2 + x_3 + \cdots + x_n}{n}.$$

    Note: The mean for a "whole" population uses the Greek letter μ (mu) as
    opposed to the symbol $\bar{x}$, pronounced "x-bar," for the mean of a "sample"
    of the population.

2. The *median* is the middle of the set of numbers. If there are an odd number
    of points, the median is the data point for which there are as many data
    points greater as there are less than that point. If there are an even number
    of points, the median is the average of the two middle numbers.

3. *Mode* is the number that occurs most frequently in a set of data. In small
    samples, there may not be a mode since nothing may repeat.

Ask students to illustrate the measures of central tendency, by using the closing prices from the following sample of Starbucks data from Yahoo! Finance, for
the week ending July 22, 2005. (You might want to mention that Starbucks was

named in honor of the coffee-loving first mate in Herman Melville's classic, *Moby Dick.*)

Students should give the answers that follow.

NOTE: When finding the measures of central tendency, some students may need to be reminded to write numbers in ascending order since they are easier to analyze in that form. In our example,

$$51.32, 51.61, 51.62, 52.03, 52.35$$

Starbucks Corp (SBUX)

Date	Open	High	Low	Close	Volume
22-Jul-05	51.58	52.03	51.23	51.32	2,381,500
21-Jul-05	51.85	52.03	51.00	51.62	2,075,900
20-Jul-05	51.50	52.22	51.32	52.03	2,668,400
19-Jul-05	52.21	52.49	51.40	51.61	2,931,200
18-Jul-05	52.43	52.51	52.13	52.35	1,859,400

SOURCE: Reproduced with permission of Yahoo! Inc. © 2006 by Yahoo! Inc. YAHOO! and the YAHOO! logo are trademarks of Yahoo! Inc.

1. The mean is

$$\bar{x} = \frac{51.32 + 51.61 + 51.62 + 52.03 + 52.35}{5} = \$51.79$$

(rounded to the nearest cent).

2. The median of the data is $51.62 since there are two data points above it and two below it:

$$51.32, \ 51.61, \ 51.62, \ 52.03, \ 52.35$$

3. The mode is the number that occurs most frequently in a set of data. Our sample has no mode since no data point is repeated. If we were using a larger sample or an entire population, then the probability of a mode existing would be high since data points would likely repeat.

Practice

Imagine a company has nine regular employees with salaries of $30,000 a year and a supervisor (tenth employee) earning $130,000 a year.

1. If you were considering taking a job with the company and wanted to find out about what salary to expect and could know just one measure of central tendency, which would you want to know? Why?

2. If you were a recruiting officer for the company and wanted to make a good impression on a prospective employee, which measure would you use? Why?

Practice Answers

1. I would want to know the mode since it gives me the salary that most people make, $30,000.

2. I would use the mean since the supervisor's salary would make the typical salary seem greater than it is (30,000 times 9 + 130,000 divided by 10 = $40,000.)

Extension

Ask students to give you other instances of one measure of central tendency being more valuable to know than the others. For example, housing prices in a particular town are best described by the median since a few very expensive or a few very inexpensive houses can dramatically change the mean, but the median will let you know that an equal number of houses are priced below and above that price.

Part B: Bell-Shaped Curve and Standard Deviation

Discussion and Questions

Tell students that when we study the stock market as a whole, we focus on how the market increases or decreases, as a percent, over a long period of time. These historical data can usually be fit to a bell-shaped curve, or what is often called the normal curve. We then can use something called standard deviation to project into the future by determining how risky a certain investment may be.

A bell-shaped curve is illustrated below. The numbers on the horizontal axis represent how far data are from the median (marked as 0) in terms of standard deviations. The shaded areas represent the percent of data that can be expected to appear in that area.

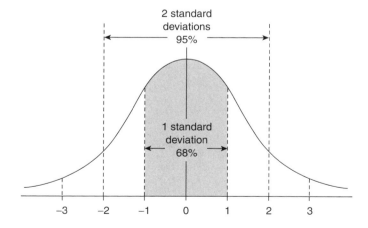

The shading shows that most of the data are "bunched" in the middle. In fact, there is a 68% probability that data points will fall within "1 standard deviation" of the median.

Calculating Standard Deviation

Tell students that you are going to show them how to calculate standard deviation by using the following data: **12, 15, 18, 23, 27** (mean equals 19). It is a small sample, and small samples usually do not fit a bell-shaped curve. However, we are going to use it to help illustrate calculation of a standard deviation and how it is related to the bell-shaped curve before we give a full-blown example where the data actually do fit the curve.

Give students the formula for standard deviation, *s:*

$$s = \sqrt{\sum \frac{(x_i - \bar{x})^2}{n - 1}}.$$

Admit that it looks complicated, but tell them that if they know what the symbols mean, it's a piece of cake. So, define them:

- $\sum$ is the Greek letter sigma and represents the sum of all possible terms for the expression that follows it (for simplicity, we did not use the index, or counter, below the sigma sign).
- x_i is the value of any data point (when the subscript i is replaced with 1, we have x_1, which is the first data point; replaced with 2, we have x_2, which is the second term, etc.).
- $\bar{x}$ is the mean of the data.
- n is the number of data points.

NOTE: The standard deviation for a whole population uses the Greek letter σ (small sigma) as opposed to the symbol s, for sample mean, and uses a divisor of n rather than $n - 1$. The divisor of $n - 1$ is used for small samples because the resultant quotient is a better indicator of how far data are from the mean.

To calculate the standard deviation using our limited data, first, find $\sqrt{\sum \frac{(x_i - \bar{x})^2}{n-1}}$ for $i = 1$ through 5, where $\bar{x} = 19$ and $n = 5$:

$$\frac{(x_1 - 19)^2}{5 - 1} + \frac{(x_2 - 19)^2}{5 - 1} + \frac{(x_3 - 19)^2}{5 - 1} + \frac{(x_4 - 19)^2}{5 - 1} + \frac{(x_5 - 19)^2}{5 - 1}$$

$$\frac{(12 - 19)^2}{5 - 1} + \frac{(15 - 19)^2}{5 - 1} + \frac{(18 - 19)^2}{5 - 1} + \frac{(23 - 19)^2}{5 - 1} + \frac{(27 - 19)^2}{5 - 1}$$

$$= \frac{146}{4} = 36.5.$$

Then, take the square root of the sum:

$$s = \sqrt{\sum \frac{(x_i - \bar{x})^2}{n - 1}} = \sqrt{36.5} = 6.0415 \text{ or } 6 \text{ (rounded)}.$$

This is the standard deviation for the data sample. If this was a valid sample for a bell-shaped curve, it could then be said that "the standard deviation of the data points is 6."

To see this visually, we turn back to our "bell-shaped curve" and note the average and the upper and lower limits of one standard deviation.

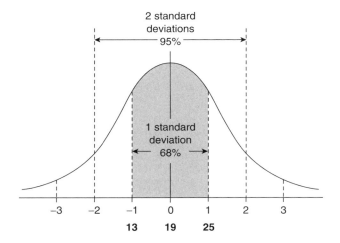

- The mean is the "0" point in the normal curve, shown above, that, in our sample, has the value 19.
- The standard deviation is marked by the two points of "−1" and "1." In our sample, these values are 13 (19 minus 6 equals 13) and 25 (19 plus 6 equals 25).
- The shaded area under the curve is about 68% of the total area under the curve, and it represents the probability that data are within 1 standard deviation of the mean. Assuming that our data are a representative sample, about 68% of the time, the price of the data would range from 13 to 25.
- Two standard deviations are marked by the two points "−2" and "2." This means that the interval between −2 and 2 contains all of the points within 2 standard deviations of the mean. In our example, the points between −2 and 2 denote prices that are within 12 points (6 times 2) of the mean. As indicated in the graph above, the probability that prices will fall within this range, 7 to 31, is about 95%.
- Three standard deviations are marked by the two points "−3" and "3." This means that the interval between −3 and 3 contains all of the points within 3 standard deviations of the mean. So, in our example, the points in that interval are within 18 points of 19, the mean. The probability that prices will fall within this range, 1 to 37, is about 99.5%.

NOTE: The empirical rule states that 68% of normally distributed data fall within 1 standard deviation of the mean, 95% fall within 2 standard deviations of the mean, and 99.5% fall within 3 standard deviations of the mean. However, in this small sample, the 95% and 99.5% may fall outside the actual data points, as is the case in this example. This illustrates the weakness of using such a small sample, which we did only for purposes of showing the calculations.

Example: S&P 500

Tell students that you are now ready to look at one of the most important applications of the bell-shaped curve, the S&P 500. The S&P 500 (the largest companies) keeps track of the average stock price of 500 companies over many years. The table below shows S&P data from 1930 through 2005, grouped by decade.

S&P 500 by Decades							
1930s		1940s		1950s		1960s	
1930	−24.9%	1940	−9.8%	1950	31.7%	1960	0.5%
1931	−43.3%	1941	−11.6%	1951	24.0%	1961	26.9%
1932	−8.2%	1942	20.3%	1952	18.4%	1962	−8.7%
1933	54.0%	1943	25.9%	1953	−1.0%	1963	22.8%
1934	−1.4%	1944	19.8%	1954	52.6%	1964	16.5%
1935	47.7%	1945	36.4%	1955	31.6%	1965	12.5%
1936	33.9%	1946	−8.1%	1956	6.6%	1966	−10.1%
1937	−35.0%	1947	5.7%	1957	−10.8%	1967	24.0%
1938	31.1%	1948	5.5%	1958	43.4%	1968	11.1%
1939	−0.4%	1949	18.8%	1959	12.0%	1969	−8.5%
1970s		1980s		1990s		2000s	
1970	4.0%	1980	32.4%	1990	−3.2%	2000	−9.1%
1971	14.3%	1981	−4.9%	1991	30.6%	2001	−11.9%
1972	19.0%	1982	21.4%	1992	7.7%	2002	−22.1%
1973	−14.7%	1983	22.5%	1993	10.0%	2003	28.7%
1974	−26.5%	1984	6.3%	1994	1.3%	2004	10.9%
1975	37.2%	1985	32.2%	1995	37.4%	2005	4.8%
1976	23.8%	1986	18.5%	1996	23.1%	2006	15.6%
1977	−7.2%	1987	5.2%	1997	33.4%		
1978	6.6%	1988	16.8%	1998	28.6%		
1979	18.4%	1989	31.5%	1999	21.0%		

SOURCE: Data provided by Standard & Poor's at www.standardandpoors.com.

If you calculate the mean and standard deviation of all these returns, you would get approximately the following:

S&P 500	
Mean	12%
Standard deviation	20%

The mean of 12% is the *average return* from 1930 through the end of 2006. That is, 12 cents was earned on every dollar invested. It's hard to believe that given the negative numbers during the Depression in the 1930s or in some recent years, the return is so high. However, those negatives are offset by years with high returns such as those in the 1980s and 1990s. This is also why you can't use a limited period of time to get useful statistical measures. Because we have used a long period of time, we can use these measures in a meaningful way. Specifically, we can use this average return of 12% to project forward. In other words, we can say that investments in the S&P 500 should provide us with a return of about 12% per year, in the long term.

The measurement of the standard deviation indicates that the average volatility or *risk* since 1930 up to the present was 20%. What does this mean? We can use the return (mean) and risk (standard deviation) to say that 68% of the time, S&P 500 investment will be worth between a low of −8% (12% − 20%) and a high of +32% (12% + 20%). Can you see just by looking at the table that most of the returns are confined to this range? That's the usefulness of the standard deviation. It tells us the usual range of returns.

The caveat is that you can project this forward only over a long period of time, usually 10 years or longer. That's when there should be enough time for ups and downs to even out to about 12%.

In general, an investor wants to maximize the return and minimize the risk. This is hard to do, but if we can compare the same time period and the same statistics, it allows us to decide which investment we might select going forward.

The following chart shows a comparison of the S&P 500 with a mythical Company X:

S&P 500		Company X	
Mean (return)	12%	Mean (return)	18%
Standard deviation (risk)	20%	Standard deviation (risk)	15%

Having the S&P 500 figures as a basis, investors can compare a company's risk and return over any time period.

In this hypothetical example, Company X would be a better investment because it has a higher return and a lower risk.

However, a company can have a good performance over a short period of time, so the caution here is this: Will the company outperform over the long term? Many companies can reach a point of maturity, and then their stock price reaches a plateau and even decreases.

Practice

Provide students with the S&P 500 sheet for this practice.

1. Our country was in a Depression during the 1930s. How do the S&P 500 returns reflect this?

2. Which decade had the least risk? The greatest risk?

3. Which decade had the least return? The greatest return?

4. If you had to choose one decade in which to invest, which would it be?

5. Research the stock prices of three publicly traded companies that interest you, then
   a. Calculate the risk and return for each company over the longest common time period available to you.

b. If you could buy only one of these stocks, which would it be? Why?

6. Assume that the three graphs below are all normal curves so that the area under each curve is the same. Assume too that each graph represents a different stock, A, B, or C.

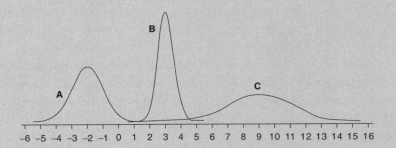

Rank each stock in order of return, risk, and best investment.

7. The graph below shows the "standard" normal curve. On the same set of axes, sketch a normal curve with the same mean but a larger standard deviation and then the same mean and a smaller standard deviation.

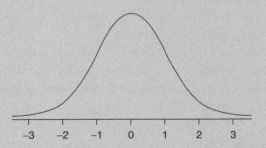

Practice Answers

1. With several sharp declines. However, there were also some years when the stock market was up sharply. In general, the 1930s were marked by high volatility.

2. Without the actual calculation of standard deviation by decade, it would be hard to say.

3. The least return was probably the 1930s. The greatest returns were probably the 1950s, 1980s, and 1990s.

4. 1990s.

5. This could be a class or group project.

6. Stock C has the highest return since it is higher in general. Stock C also is the highest risk because it is spread out more (larger standard

deviation). Stock C would also be the best investment because it has the highest return.

7. The graph below shows the original curve, B, along with Graph A with a smaller standard deviation (less spread) and Graph C with a larger standard deviation (more spread).

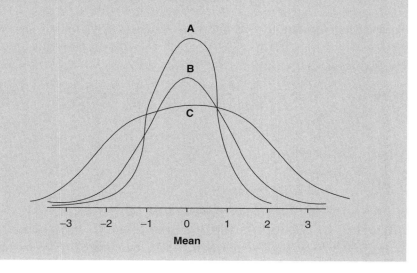

Extension

The equation for the "standard" bell-shaped curve is $y = \frac{1}{\sqrt{2\pi}} e^{-\frac{z^2}{2}}$, where z is the number of standard deviations and y is the height of the curve.

a. Use a graphing utility to sketch this graph.
b. What does the value on the horizontal axis represent where $z = 0$?
c. What happens to the curve when the absolute value of $z = 1$? Why do you think that happens?
d. What is the maximum height of this "standard" normal curve?

TEACHING EXAMPLE 4.4

Statistics of Stock II: Weighted Average,
Correlation, Line of Best Fit

NCTM Content Standards

Numbers and Operations; Algebra; Data Analysis; Probability

Process Standards

Problem Solving; Reasoning and Proof; Communication; Connections; Representation

Money Applications

Students will

- Calculate weighted averages
- Calculate standard deviations of multiple sets of data
- Calculate correlation
- Calculate line of best fit

Discussion and Questions

Tell students that this activity contains four important mathematical concepts that they will apply to investments. The four are weighted average, correlations, standard deviation of a combined portfolio, and the line of best fit (also known as the line of regression).

These calculations get at the following maxim: "Don't put all of your eggs in one basket." But how can you implement this strategy? Most people know that putting their money in just one investment is too risky, so they diversify their investments. This means they divide their investment money among various investments in what is called a "combined portfolio" to minimize their risk and maximize their return.

We take this simple strategy and lay it out step-by-step mathematically. First we learn to calculate a weighted average.

Example A: Weighted Average

Suppose a person puts his or her money into three different types of investments, say, stocks, bonds, and money market accounts. What would be the overall return and risk of his or her combined portfolio?

Portfolio	Return	Risk
Stocks	12%	20%
Bonds	6%	9%
Money market accounts	4%	3%

The "return" part of the problem is somewhat simple. We calculate a "weighted average," which is mathematically straightforward. The "risk," however, is a problem because the mathematics is quite challenging and will be presented in Example C below.

To calculate a weighted average, multiply each investment's weight by its return, then add the results. For example, suppose that the portfolio above is weighted as follows:

50% of S&P 500 with a return of 12%
30% of bonds with a return of 6%
20% of money market accounts with a return of 4%

The weighted average is calculated by multiplying each investment percentage (the weighting) by the return for that investment. For instance, the weight of the first investment, the S&P 500 mutual fund, is 50% (meaning that 50% of the portfolio is invested in the S&P 500). This percentage is multiplied by its anticipated return of 12%. The result is the "contribution" made by that investment—in this case, 6% (50% times 12% equals 6%).

This is calculated for all three of the investments (or however many investments there are in the portfolio).

The expression for a weighted average is

$$\sum w_i r_i,$$

where

w = the weight of an investment
r = the expected return of that investment

The weighted average for this portfolio is thus the following sum: $.50 \times .12 + .30 \times .06 + .20 \times .04 = 0.086$, or 8.6%.

Thus, the return of this portfolio is expected to be 8.6% over the long term (10 years or more).

Example B: Data Correlation

For our next step in constructing a combined portfolio, we have to calculate the correlation between investments. Mathematically, we have to determine the number, r, that quantifies a correlation relationship.

To understand correlation, have students consider these three scatter diagrams:

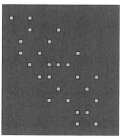
Diagram A

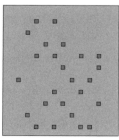
Diagram B

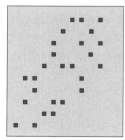
Diagram C

Ask students the following questions:

1. Does Diagram A show any apparent trend? Describe.

2. Does Diagram B show any apparent trend? Describe.

3. How does Diagram C differ from Diagram B? Describe.

Answers:

1. Yes, it's a decreasing or negative correlation.

2. No, it appears to be random.

3. Yes, it's an increasing correlation or shows a positive correlation.

When the data are organized as a trend, as in Diagrams A (negative) and C (positive), we can say that the data are correlated. Diagram B appears not to be correlated and, in fact, shows a random scattering of the data.

If the data are organized showing an upward trend (Diagram C), we say that the data are positively correlated. If they show a downward trend (Diagram A), the data are negatively correlated.

Correlation, designated as r, is quantified as a number from -1 to $+1$. If the data were exactly negatively correlated, r would equal -1. If there were no correlation, r would be 0. If the data were perfectly correlated, r would be $+1$.

Furthermore, as a general rule, if a correlation is 0.8 and above, it is said that the data are highly correlated. If it is 0.3 and below, it is said that the data have a low correlation.

Let's look at two stocks, Wendy's and McDonald's, for an 8-day period in August 2004.

Date	Wendy's	McDonald's
August 16, 2004	$32.90	$25.70
August 17, 2004	$33.03	$25.80
August 28, 2004	$33.81	$26.37
August 19, 2004	$34.35	$26.46
August 20, 2004	$34.23	$26.46
August 23, 2004	$34.85	$27.07
August 24, 2004	$34.69	$26.60
August 25, 2004	$34.85	$26.84

We can first draw a scatter diagram with vertical values representing McDonald's stock prices and horizontal values representing Wendy's stock prices. Is a trend apparent—that is, do you think the stock prices are correlated?

By eyeballing the data, there appears to be a positive correlation. Finding r will give us a better idea of how good that correlation is, so let's calculate a correlation between two investments:

$r=$ the correlation or, more precisely, the "correlation coefficient."

Although there are several variations of the formula, we'll use one that makes the calculation somewhat easy:

$$r = \frac{n\sum(xy) - (\sum x)(\sum y)}{\sqrt{[n\sum x^2 - (\sum x)^2][n\sum y^2 - (\sum y)^2]}}.$$

It doesn't look very easy, but if you organize the variables, it's quite manageable.

First, we set up a table for each term, letting x represent Wendy's and y, McDonald's:

	x	x^2	y	y^2	xy
1	32.90	1,082.41	25.70	660.49	845.53
2	33.03	1,090.98	25.80	665.64	852.17
3	33.81	1,143.12	26.37	695.38	891.57
4	34.35	1,179.92	26.46	700.13	908.90
5	34.23	1,171.69	26.46	700.13	905.73
6	34.85	1,214.52	27.07	732.78	943.39
7	34.69	1,203.40	26.60	707.56	922.75
8	34.85	1,214.52	26.84	720.39	935.37
Σ	272.71	9,300.56	211.30	5,582.50	7,205.41

Second, we substitute the appropriate numbers in the following formula:

$$r = \frac{8(7,205.41) - (272.71)(211.30)}{\sqrt{[8(9,300.56) - (272.71)^2][8(5,582.50) - (211.30)^2]}}.$$

$r = .96.$

We could have used a calculator to get r, but we think that if students see how this number is actually calculated, they will have a better understanding of correlation and, certainly, a greater appreciation of what their calculator can do!

The correlation is almost perfect, at .96. The stock of McDonald's and Wendy's during the 8 days of the data can be said to be very highly correlated. So, the stocks performed in a similar way—for example, when one stock increased in price, the other did too.

Now, let's return to the portfolio. The following table shows the correlations for each investment along with the return and standard deviations:

			Correlations		
Portfolio (Weights)	Return	Risk	Stocks	Bonds	Money Market
Stocks (50%)	12%	20%	1.00		
Bonds (30%)	6%	9%	0.15	1.00	
Money market accounts (20%)	4%	3%	−0.05	0.24	1.00

It shows that the correlation between stocks and bonds is 0.15, or a very low correlation. The correlation between stocks and money market accounts is −0.05, slightly negatively correlated. The correlation between bonds and money market accounts is 0.24, or quite low.

With this correlation information, we are now ready to calculate the "risk" of a combined portfolio, or standard deviation of a combined portfolio.

Example C: Standard Deviation of a Combined Portfolio

The calculation of the standard deviation of a combined portfolio uses a somewhat involved formula:

$$s_{portfolio} = \sqrt{\sum w_i w_j s_i s_j r_{ij}}.$$

Let's define each part of this formula:

Σ is the Greek letter sigma and represents the sum of all possible terms for the expression that follows it (for simplicity, we did not use the index, or counter, that usually appears below the sigma sign).

w is the weight. Specifically, w_i is the weight of one of the investments, and w_j is the weight of another investment.

s is the standard deviation. Specifically, s_i is the standard deviation of one of the investments, and s_j is the weight of another investment.

r_{ij} is the correlation between two investments.

Repeating our data for the combined portfolio, we perform the following calculation:

			Correlations		
Portfolio (Weights)	Return	Risk	Stocks	Bonds	Money Market
Stocks (50%)	12%	20%	1.00		
Bonds (30%)	6%	9%	0.15	1.00	
Money market accounts (20%)	4%	3%	−0.05	0.24	1.00

$$s_{portfolio} = \sqrt{\sum w_i w_j s_i s_j r_{ij}}.$$

First, every possible term of the series is calculated:

	Stocks	Bonds	Money Market Accounts
Stocks	(.50)(.50)(.20) (.20)(1) = **0.01**	(.50)(.30)(.20)(0.09) (0.15) = **0.000405**	(.50)(.20)(.20)(0.03) (−0.05) = **−0.00003**
Bonds	(.50)(.30)(.20)(.09) (0.15) = **0.000405**	(.30)(.30)(0.09)(0.09) (1) = **0.000729**	(.30)(.20)(0.09)(0.03) (0.24) = **0.0000388**
Money market accounts	(.50)(.20)(.20)(0.03) (−0.05) = **−0.00003**	(.30)(.20)(.09)(.03) (.24) = **0.0000388**	(.20)(.20)(.03)(.03) (1) = **0.000036**

Now, we sum each term in the above table, the numbers in bold, and take the square root. Because we have two negative numbers, we can sum the positive numbers and then subtract the negative ones:

$$s_{portfolio} = \sqrt{.01165 - .00006},$$
$$s_{portfolio} = \sqrt{.01159},$$
$$s_{portfolio} = .107 \text{ or } 10.7\%.$$

Our combined portfolio has a return of 8.6%, as determined in Example A, with a risk of 10.7%. This means that there is 68% (remember the empirical rule) probability that the return on the portfolio will be between a loss of about 2% (10.7 minus 8.6 equals 2.1) and a gain of over 19% (10.7 plus 8.6 equals 19.3).

These measures can then be compared to other portfolios with their returns and risks. Just as we saw before, the return and risk of an individual stock, or mutual fund, is not very meaningful all by itself. It needs to be compared to an alternative.

Example D: The Line of Best Fit

Our last step in working with a combined portfolio is to construct a line of best fit, a regression, or the line of least squares. They are different names for the same mathematical process.

Why is this helpful for investments? It allows us to project prices forward through a formula. It also allows us an opportunity to use algebra and the formula for a line.

Let's return to our scatter diagram for Wendy's and McDonald's. This time, let's actually calculate the line of best fit for the data. Here again are the data and the scatter diagram:

Date	Wendy's	McDonald's
August 16, 2004	$32.90	$25.70
August 17, 2004	$33.03	$25.80
August 18, 2004	$33.81	$26.37
August 19, 2004	$34.35	$26.46
August 20, 2004	$34.23	$26.46
August 23, 2004	$34.85	$27.07
August 24, 2004	$34.69	$26.60
August 25, 2004	$34.85	$26.84

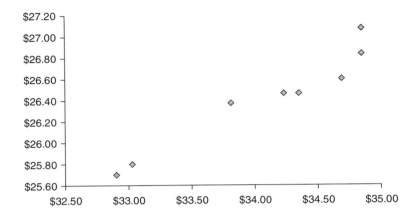

We could begin by approximating the line of best fit by hand. Here are two such hand-drawn lines, *l* and *m:*

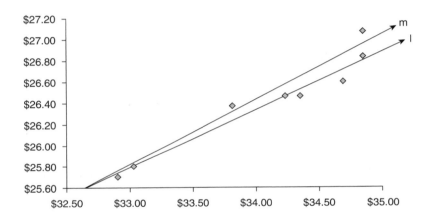

These are only "eyeballed." We can do better, by using the principle of least squares to find the line that "best" fits the data.

We start with the slope-intercept form of the straight line:

$$y = mx + b,$$

where

$$m = \frac{\sum xy - \frac{(\sum x \sum y)}{n}}{\sum x^2 - \frac{(\sum x)^2}{n}}.$$

We now calculate *m* using the values in the table that we used in Example B when calculating the correlation, *r:*

	x	x^2	y	y^2	xy
1	32.90	1,082.41	25.70	660.49	845.53
2	33.03	1,090.98	25.80	665.64	852.17
3	33.81	1,143.12	26.37	695.38	891.57
4	34.35	1,179.92	26.46	700.13	908.90
5	34.23	1,171.69	26.46	700.13	905.73
6	34.85	1,214.52	27.07	732.78	943.39
7	34.69	1,203.40	26.60	707.56	922.75
8	34.85	1,214.52	26.84	720.39	935.37
Σ	272.71	9,300.56	211.30	5,582.50	7,205.41

$$m = \frac{7,205.41 - \frac{(272.71)(211.30)}{8}}{9,300.56 - \frac{(272.71)^2}{8}}.$$

$$m = .589.$$

Having this value for m, we can now find the value of b.

$$b = \bar{y} - m\bar{x}.$$

$$b = \frac{211.30}{8} - .589\frac{272.71}{8}.$$

$$b = 6.33.$$

The straight line that represents the best fit line of Wendy's and McDonald's is therefore

$$y = .589x + 6.33.$$

We can now use this line for projections, but first let's see if we can verify that the line is correct, which is itself a projection. To check this formula by estimating, let's say that if Wendy's price was $40, what would McDonald's be?

$$y = .589(40) + 6.33.$$

$$y = 29.89.$$

This looks right. If Wendy's is $40, then McDonald's should be around $30. From the table, it appears that McDonald's has a price of about $10 more than Wendy's.

Practice

1. Calculate, by hand, the standard deviation of a combined portfolio of the following two investments:

		Correlations		
Portfolio (Weights)	Return	Risk	A	B
Investment A (70%)	6%	15%	1	
Investment B (30%)	10%	25%	0.30	1

2. For the following data, prepare a scatter diagram and calculate the correlation.

Date	Company A	Company B
September 12, 2005	$16.12	$47.50
September 13, 2005	$16.37	$47.83
September 14, 2005	$15.90	$46.99
September 15, 2005	$17.05	$45.15
September 16, 2005	$17.11	$43.67

3. Calculate the equation of the line of best fit for the following data:

Date	Company X	Company Y
September 12, 2005	$11.14	$33.21
September 13, 2005	$10.55	$33.89
September 14, 2005	$10.32	$34.05
September 15, 2005	$9.19	$35.53
September 16, 2005	$9.88	$36.49

4. Verify the accuracy of the equation by a projection.

Practice Answers

1. The standard deviation of the two investments is.... Using our formula and inserting the data, we first calculate every term:

$$s_{portfolio} = \sqrt{\sum w_i w_j s_i s_j r_{ij}}.$$

	Investment A	Investment B
Investment A	$w_1 w_1 s_1 s_1 r_{1,1}$ $= (.70)(.70)(.15)(.15)(1)$ **$= 0.011025$**	$w_1 w_2 s_1 s_2 r_{1,2}$ $= (.70)(.30)(.15)(.25)(.30)$ **$= 0.005513$**
Investment B	$w_1 w_2 s_1 s_2 r_{1,2}$ $= (.70)(.30)(.15)(.25)(.30)$ **$= 0.005513$**	$w_2 w_2 s_2 s_2 r_{2,2}$ $= (.30)(.30)(.25)(.25)(1)$ **$= 0.005625$**

Now, we sum each term in the above table, the numbers in bold, and take the square root. Since there are no negative numbers, we can simply sum the four numbers:

$$s_{portfolio} = \sqrt{.02768},$$

$$s_{portfolio} = .166,$$

or about 16.6%.

The combined portfolio, then, has a risk of about 6%.

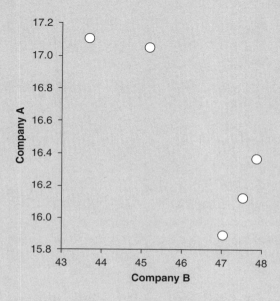

2. The correlation is calculated as

$$r = \frac{n \sum (xy) - (\sum x)(\sum y)}{\sqrt{[n \sum x^2 - (\sum x)^2][n \sum y^2 - (\sum y)^2]}}.$$

Entering the data:

	X	x^2	y	y^2	xy
1	16.12	259.85	47.50	2,256.25	765.70
2	16.37	267.98	47.83	2,287.71	782.98
3	15.90	252.81	46.99	2,208.06	747.14
4	17.05	290.70	45.15	2,038.52	769.81
5	17.11	292.75	43.67	1,907.07	747.19
Σ	82.55	1,364.09	231.14	10,697.61	3,812.82

Then, we substitute the appropriate numbers in the following formula:

$$r = \frac{5(3,812.82) - (82.55)(231.14)}{\sqrt{[5(1,364.09) - (82.55)^2][5(10,697.61) - (231.14)^2]}}.$$

$$r = -.85.$$

Thus, the correlation is highly negatively correlated. That is, as one stock goes up, the other goes down.

3. Start with the equation for a straight line:

Equation for a line: $y = mx + b$,

where

$$m = \frac{\sum xy - \frac{(\sum x \sum y)}{n}}{\sum x^2 - \frac{(\sum x)^2}{n}}.$$

We now calculate m using the data given, repeated here:

Date	Company X	Company Y
September 12, 2005	$11.14	$33.21
September 13, 2005	$10.55	$33.89
September 14, 2005	$10.32	$34.05
September 15, 2005	$9.19	$35.53
September 16, 2005	$9.88	$36.49

First, we construct a table of values:

	X	x^2	y	y^2	xy
1	11.14	124.10	33.21	1,102.90	369.96
2	10.55	111.30	33.89	1,148.53	357.54
3	10.32	106.50	34.05	1,159.40	351.40
4	9.19	84.46	35.53	1,262.38	326.52
5	9.88	97.61	36.49	1,331.52	360.52
Σ	51.08	523.97	173.17	6,004.73	1,765.94

$$m = \frac{1,765.94 - \frac{(51.08)(173.17)}{5}}{523.97 - \frac{(51.08)^2}{5}}.$$

$$m = -1.48.$$

Having this value for m, we can now find the value of b.

$$b = \bar{y} - m\bar{x}.$$

$$b = \frac{173.17}{5} - (-1.48)\frac{51.08}{5}.$$
$$b = 49.75.$$

The straight line that represents the line of best fit for these data is therefore

$$y = -1.48x + 49.75.$$

4. We can now use this line for projections.
   If $x = 5$, what is y?

$$y = -1.48(5) + 49.75.$$
$$y = 42.35.$$

This looks right. If Company X was 5, then it appears from the table that Company Y would be around 40, or so.

Extension

Have the students track the prices of two stocks over a 2-week period (or whatever period you prefer). Have them construct a data table and scatter diagram of the two stock prices. Then have them calculate the correlation, r, between the two stocks. Then have them calculate the line of best fit for the two stocks using the formula for a line. Finally, have them project a price for one of the stocks given a projected price of the other stock.

5

Buying a House
Versus Renting

How Much Will It Cost?

Home ownership is one of the cornerstones of wealth . . .
—Roger Ferguson, Vice Chairman, Federal Reserve Board

Buying a home is the most common way for Americans to accumulate wealth. Therefore, applying math to real estate can be very helpful to students. The applications in this chapter address a number of National Council of Teachers of Mathematics (NCTM) standards.

NCTM STANDARDS APPLIED IN THIS CHAPTER

Content

- *Number and Operations.* Understand meanings of operations and how they relate to one another; compute fluently and make reasonable estimates.
- *Algebra.* Understand patterns, relations, and functions; represent and analyze mathematical situations and structures using algebraic symbols; use mathematical models to represent and understand quantitative relationships.

Process

- Problem Solving; Reasoning and Proof; Communication; Connections; Representation

BACKGROUND: BASICS OF BUYING A HOUSE AND RENTING AN APARTMENT

In America, one of the most common ways to accumulate wealth is through home ownership. It builds wealth in two ways: through the "forced savings" of paying down a mortgage and through appreciation—the rise in a home's value over time. In addition, the federal government subsidizes home ownership by giving a mortgage interest deduction, so if you itemize deductions, you pay less taxes.

The sooner you own real estate, the earlier you can start building equity and the better your opportunity to accumulate wealth. Here is a recent chart from the federal government that illustrates the difference that home ownership can make.

Table 5.1 Average Net Worth of Homeowners Versus Renters

Annual Income	*Owners*	*Renters*
$80,000 and up	$451,200	$87,400
$50,000 to $79,999	$194,610	$25,000
$30,000 to $49,999	$126,500	$10,600
$16,000 to $29,999	$112,600	$4,240
Under $16,000	$73,000	$500

SOURCE: VIP Forum, Federal Reserve Board.

Buying a house is as much a lifestyle decision as it is a money decision. One of the problems in deciding whether to rent or buy is that usually we are comparing two different things. That is, we usually don't find an equivalent house to rent and compare it to the actual purchasing of that same house. We usually compare a garden apartment to a house on a cul-de-sac. Both may be nice, but they are not the same.

Furthermore, we don't compare all the costs. After buying a house, there are shrubs to replace, grass to cut, siding to repaint, and driveways to repair, just to mention a few items. Renting doesn't come with these additional expenses.

Since it is difficult to compare renting and buying, and most people would prefer to buy, here are two critical questions to ask to solve this dilemma in a practical way:

- How badly do you want to buy a house?
- Can you afford the costs of buying and maintaining the house you want?

If you really want to buy a house, then you will probably find a way to do it, even if you have to compromise. That is, if you cannot afford the house you want but you still want to buy, then you need to consider buying a less expensive place or perhaps purchase a condo or co-op. If not, then rent.

Co-ops are often the form of ownership in cities, where a person owns only a percentage of a building and not a particular unit per se, strange as that may seem. With condos, found in urban and suburban areas, a person usually owns only the inside of the specific unit they purchase.

Yes, the value of houses (and condos and co-ops) generally increases over time, and this is a good reason to buy. In fact, there are times when real estate investments have increased by a considerable amount. For instance, in 2005, the U.S. average increase in housing prices was 13%. But there were other years when the value of houses was flat or, even in some years, when they actually decreased. On average, however, houses increase about 5% to 7% a year, but this depends on three things: location, location, and location. A desirable location in terms of such things as proximity to work and quality of schools can mean a very good return on a real estate investment.

Renting, on the other hand, has a number of advantages. First, renting can suit people just starting their careers. Second, renting is almost always cheaper than buying. Third, a person may not have enough for a down payment to buy a house. These are all reasons to rent rather than buy.

When you add it all up, then, the decision to buy could provide a desirable lifestyle and an increasing value to your financial assets. However, the critical question remains: Can you afford to buy and maintain a house for the long term?

Banks and mortgage companies have a way to figure this out for you. They will give you a mortgage only if the mortgage payment, real estate taxes, and home insurance are within 28% of your gross income. Also, when added to your other debt payments, total debt service must be within 36% of your income.

Since most people don't have enough money to buy a house outright, we use mortgages. The most common type is a fixed-rate 30-year mortgage. You pay the same amount each month for 30 years, and when the mortgage is paid up, you own the house free and clear!

There are variations on this type of mortgage. There are 25-year or 15-year mortgages with, of course, higher monthly payments. There are also adjustable-rate mortgages (ARMs), which have fluctuating rates, usually adjusted on an annual basis to reflect changes in the prime interest rate. The advantage of this type of mortgage is that the initial rate is usually quite low; the disadvantage is that rates can rise so much that you can no longer afford your house.

One of the biggest numbers to overcome is the amount of down payment you need to get a mortgage. Traditionally, you needed a down payment of 25% of the value of the house. In the case of a condo, you sometimes need as little as 5%. Recently, some banks and mortgage companies have relaxed these rules because of anticipated increases in real estate values. Some banks have even offered zero-down mortgages because they have assumed that the value of the house will increase nicely. Common, however, is that if your down payment is less than 20%, you are usually required to purchase a private mortgage insurance (PMI) policy. This typically can cost from $250 to $1,200 a year.

Perhaps the nicest term in housing is equity. That's how much of the house or condo you actually own. As a homeowner, it's what's yours at any point in time. Initially, the down payment is your equity. As the principal is paid off or the house increases in value, then the amount of homeowner equity increases. You are richer!

TEACHING EXAMPLE 5.1

Budgeting for a Down Payment

NCTM Content Standards

Numbers and Operations; Algebra

Process Standards

Problem Solving; Connections

Money Applications

Students will

- Calculate future value of savings over time
- Determine the value of a house or condo for which a down payment is sufficient

Our Dream Condo

Price = $320,000

2 Bedroom Condo

Top Floor

Breathtaking Views

New Kitchen

Health Club

1,155 sq.ft.

Photo by Ashley Westbrook.

Discussion and Questions

Ask students to imagine that they are married and that in 5 years, they and their spouse would like to buy a condo in the city like the one described in this ad. Assume the following:

- Their budget is as given below and remains about the same over the 5 years.
- They have no savings now.
- They dedicate all their savings to a down payment.
- Their bank would require a down payment of 25% for a mortgage.

In 5 years, how much of a down payment will they have for a condo if

a. They keep their saving under their mattress?

b. Their savings earn 5% interest compounded annually?

c. They move in with parents, pay no rent, all other expenses remain the same, and their savings earn 5%?

The married couple's income is $7,000 per month, or $84,000 a year: You will note that the $7,000 a month (or $84,000 annually) is the total or gross income. This is before taxes, the amount of which is shown in an expense category. There are also other costs, such as medical premiums that are typically deducted from one's paycheck, so although one can think of their salary, in this case, as $7,000, one would actually get less in actual cash.

Table 5.2 Budget: Married Couple

	Monthly	Annually
Income	$7,000	$84,000
Expenses		
Rent	$1,864	$22,368
Utilities	125	1,500
Telephone	150	1,800
Groceries	350	4,200
Clothing	150	1,800
Eating out	300	3,600
Car loan	1,025	12,300
Gas and maintenance	400	4,800
Insurances	225	2,700
Taxes	1,200	14,400
Miscellaneous	200	2,400
Available to save	1,011	12,132
Total Expenses	**$7,000**	**$84,000**

Solution

a. If they keep their savings under a mattress, they would have the down payment for a condo priced at about $242,640, but not for a $320,000 condo like the one in the ad. Saving $12,132 a year, in 5 years, assuming no interest, they would have accumulated $60,660 ($12,132 times 5 equals $60,660). Since $60,660 is $\frac{1}{4}$ (25%) of the total cost of the property, they have the down payment for 4 times $60,660, which is $242,640.

   We can also figure this out using a proportion. Let x represent the value of the most expensive condo they have a down payment for, then $\frac{\$60,660}{25\%} = \frac{x}{100\%}$. By converting the percents to decimal form, we get $\frac{\$60,660}{.25} = \frac{x}{1}$. So, performing the division, we get $x = \$242,640$.

b. If their savings earned 5% interest compounded annually, they would have the down payment for a condo priced at about $268,144 ($25,504 more thanks to interest!). First, apply the ordinary annuity formula, which assumes that the savings would be deposited at the end of the year, developed in Chapter 2, to get total savings.

$$FV = Pmt \frac{(1+r)^n - 1}{r},$$

where

   $FV =$ future value of savings
   $Pmt =$ the savings per year
   $r =$ interest or investment rate expressed as a decimal
   $n =$ the number of years that investment exists

Using this formula, the couple will have $67,036 after 5 years, if the annual interest rate they earned on their money was 5%, since

$$FV = \$12{,}132\frac{(1+.05)^5 - 1}{.05} = \$67{,}036.$$

If this were their 25% down payment, they would have the down payment for a condo priced at

$$4 \times \$67{,}036 = \$268{,}144.$$

c. If they move in with their parents, pay no rent, and all other expenses remain the same, they would have the down payment for a condo priced at about $762,537 (about $500,000 of which is thanks to their parents' generosity!). If they moved in with parents rent free, they could save $1,864 more a month for a total of $2,875 a month, or a whopping $34,500 a year.

   Applying the ordinary annuity formula, we get $FV = \$34{,}500$ $\frac{(1+.05)^5 - 1}{.05} = \$190{,}634$ in total savings. So, they have the down payment for a condo worth about $762,537. Wow, that's a lot of condo! Of course, a condo at that price would require that your mortgage be $571,903, which, at 7% over 30 years, would cost $3,803 per month (you'll see how this is calculated in the next teaching example). So, you and your spouse would probably not be approved for such a large loan. You could, however, buy something outright with your savings ($190,634) or buy something for which you have enough monthly income to meet the mortgage payments. But this whole strategy needs to consider factors other than money—that is, the emotional toll on parents, yourself, and children under such a living arrangement.

Practice

1. In the last problem, what value of a condo would the couple have a 25% down payment for if they earned 5% annually on their savings and
    a. they lived with their parents for only 2 years?
    b. they lived with their parents for 3 years but needed only a 15% down payment?

2. What priced home would the single person whose budget appears below have the down payment for, if this person applied all of the savings for the next 3 years (that earns 4% annually) together with $10,000 the person presently has in savings (that earns 5.5% annually) to that down payment? (Assume a 20% down payment is required.)

Practice Answers

1. a. Enough for the down payment on a condo worth $282,900. At the end of 2 years, they have $70,725 in savings: $FV = \$34{,}500\frac{(1+.05)^2 - 1}{.05} = \$70{,}725$ and $4 \times \$70{,}725 = \$282{,}900$.

Table 5.3   Budget: Single Person

	Monthly	*Annually*
Income	$2,917	$35,000
Expenses		
Rent	$850	$10,200
Utilities	100	1,200
Telephone	130	1,560
Groceries	250	3,000
Clothing	120	1,440
Eating out	150	1,800
Car loan	315	3,780
Gas and maintenance	64	768
Insurances	108	1,296
Taxes	375	4,500
Miscellaneous	105	1,260
Available to save	350	4,200
Total Expenses	**$2,917**	**$35,000 rounded**

   b. Enough for a down payment on a condo worth $725,075. At the end of 3 years, they will have $108,761.25 in savings since

$$FV = \$34,500\,\frac{(1+.05)^3-1}{.05} = \$108,761.$$ Using the proportion method to solve for x, $\frac{\$108,761}{15\%} = \frac{x}{100\%}$. The solution to which is $725,075.

2. The person would have enough in savings, $44,221, to make the 20% down payment for a home worth $221,107 since $4,200 invested at 4% for 3 years yields $13,110.72, and $10,000 invested at 5.5% for 3 years yields $31,680.25 as demonstrated below.

$$\$4,200\,\frac{(1+.04)^3-1}{.04} + \$10,000(1+.055)^3$$

$$= \$13,110.72 + \$11,742.42 = \$24,853.13$$

and

$$\$24,853.13 \times 5 = \$124,265.65.$$

Project

Determine if the single person whose budget is given above ($35,000 annual income) would qualify for a $175,000 mortgage, if the mortgage cost $1,284.50 a month, given the person's income and the rule the banks use of not exceeding 28% of the gross income for housing expenses. Assume the real estate taxes are $3,800 a year and homeowner's insurance is $300 a year.

TEACHING EXAMPLE 5.2

Determining Mortgage Payments: Tables, Formulas, Spreadsheets

NCTM Content Standards

Numbers and Operations; Algebra

Process Standards

Problem Solving; Reasoning and Proof; Communication; Connections; Representation

Money Applications

Students will

- Use tables to determine mortgage payments
- Develop and apply the formulas behind amortization tables
- Learn the spreadsheet formulas for mortgage payments in Excel

Discussion and Questions

Ask students the following:

Assuming that you have the down payment for a home, how do you find out how much a mortgage will cost?

Answer: There are several methods to determine the amount of monthly payments of a mortgage. We will review three of them: using a table, using an annuity formula, and using a spreadsheet formula.

1. Here is a mortgage table showing the monthly payment amount per thousand borrowed. To determine a specific mortgage, find the interest rate that applies and then multiply by the number of thousands borrowed.

Table 5.4   Mortgage Payments per Month per $1,000
            (Assumes a 30-Year, Fixed-Rate Mortgage)

6%	6.5%	7%	7.5%	8%
$6.00	$6.32	$6.65	$6.99	$7.34

Let's assume that you wish to determine the monthly mortgage amount for a 30-year loan of $100,000 at 7%. The amount per $1,000 for a 7% mortgage is $6.65 (as shown in the table). Since you want to borrow $100,000, multiply $6.65 by 100, getting $665. This is the monthly mortgage amount you would pay.

2. Another method to determine the monthly amount of a mortgage is to use the formula that is the basis of the table above. This formula is as follows: the present value of an ordinary annuity, with the present value the amount of the mortgage.

To get this formula, we can modify a formula that was developed in Chapter 2: the future value formula for an ordinary annuity. Let's review what that formula looked like:

$$FV_{ordinary\ annuity} = Pmt \left[\frac{(1+r)^n - 1}{r} \right],$$

where

$r =$ interest rate

We would need to modify this formula by finding the simple PV of this future value formula.

If you recall, this formula was also developed in Chapter 2, which was

$$FV = PV(1+r)^n \text{ or } PV = \frac{FV}{(1+r)^n}.$$

By using this simple PV form, we can simply divide the FV of an ordinary annuity by

$$(1+r)^n.$$

When we divide in this way, the formula for PV of an ordinary annuity would be

$$PV_{ordinary\ annuity} = Pmt \left[\frac{(1+r)^n - 1}{r} \right] \div (1+r)^n.$$

Carrying out the division, we obtain

$$PV = Pmt \frac{1 - \frac{1}{(1+r)^n}}{r} \text{ or } PV = Pmt \frac{1 - (1+r)^{-n}}{r}.$$

Because a mortgage is calculated as a *monthly* amount, we can write this formula as

$$PV = Pmt \frac{1 - \left(1 + \frac{r}{12}\right)^{-n \times 12}}{\frac{r}{12}},$$

where

$PV =$ the initial mortgage amount (present value of the mortgage)
$Pmt =$ the monthly mortgage amount
$r =$ the mortgage interest rate
$n =$ the number of years (30 years for a standard 30-year mortgage)

Finally, we can solve this formula for Pmt, so we can find the monthly payment for any mortgage.

By rearranging our formula, Pmt would be

$$Pmt = \frac{PV\left(\frac{r}{12}\right)}{1 - \left(1 + \frac{r}{12}\right)^{-n}}.$$

Using our example—a mortgage of $100,000 (*PV*), an interest rate of 7%, and the number of years equaling 30—we can solve for our monthly mortgage payment:

$$Pmt = \frac{\$100,000\left(\frac{.07}{12}\right)}{1 - \left(1 + \frac{.07}{12}\right)^{-30 \times 12}} = \$665.30.$$

This, then, is our second method of finding the monthly amount of a mortgage.

3. Our final method is with a spreadsheet program that has the formula for a monthly mortgage payment built into it. Using the Excel spreadsheet program, the formula for a mortgage is as follows (Note: All Excel formulas begin with an " = " sign.):

$$= \text{PMT(rate, nper, pv, fv, type)},$$

where

rate = interest rate per period
nper = number of periods
pv = the amount of the mortgage (present value)
fv = future value, which is left blank in our case
type = "0" in our case, which represents an ordinary annuity ("1" would designate an annuity due)

Inserting the information in the spreadsheet is as simple as inserting the specific values. Note that the percent must be divided by 12, and the 30 years has to be multiplied by 12. In our case, we enter the following:

$$= PMT(.07/12, 30^*12, 100000, 0, 0). \text{ Hit Return and get } \$665.30.$$

We can see this in the spreadsheet as follows:

	A	B	C	D	E	F	G
1	rate	nper	pv	monthly payment=PMT(0.07/12,30*12,100000)			
2	0.07/12	30*12	100000	($665.30)			

Note that in Method 1, we obtained the rounded amount of $665, whereas in Methods 2 and 3, we were able to obtain the more precise amount of $665.30.

Practice

1. Calculate the monthly payments for a 30-year mortgage of $200,000, at 8%, using Methods 1 and 2 (or 3). Which payment is greater? Why?

2. Calculate the monthly payments for a 20-year mortgage of $250,000, at 6.5%, using Method 1. Then calculate the monthly payments for Method 2 or 3. Which payment is the greater? Why?

3. When will Method 1 give the greatest amount? Explain.

4. Extend Table 5.4 to include the following rates: 4%, 4.5%, 5%, 5.5%, and 8.5%. What is an easy way to do this?

Practice Answers

1. Method 1: $1,468; Methods 2 and 3: $1,467.53. Method 1 gives the greater monthly payment because calculation of the monthly payment for a $1,000 loan was *rounded up* to get to the nearest cent.

2. Method 1: $1,580.17; Methods 2 and 3: $1,580. Methods 2 and 3 give the greater monthly payment because calculation of the monthly payment for a $1,000 loan in Method 1 was *rounded down* to get to the nearest cent.

3. Method 1 will give the greatest amount when the calculation for the monthly payment on a $1,000 loan must be rounded up.

4.

4%	4.5%	5%	5.5%	6%	6.5%	7%	7.5%	8%	8.5%
$4.77	$5.07	$5.37	$5.68	$6.00	$6.32	$6.65	$6.99	$7.34	$7.69

An efficient way to do this is use your computer or calculator to set up the problem and just change the percent.

Project: Flexing Your Algebra Muscle

Have the students derive the *PV* of an *annuity due formula* from the *FV* of annuity due, which was given in Chapter 2 as

$$FV_{annuity\ due} = Pmt\left[\frac{(1+r)^n - 1}{r}\right] \times (1+r).$$

The answer is shown below:

Recall that in Chapter 2, we also showed that $FV = PV(1+r)^n$. So by applying the transitive property of equality, we have $PV(1+r)^n = Pmt\left[\frac{(1+r)^n-1}{r}\right] \times (1+r)$. Multiplying both sides of the equation by $(1+r)^{-n}$, we now have

$$PV = Pmt\left[\frac{(1+r)^n - 1}{r}\right] \times (1+r)^{1-n}.$$

Simplifying and distributing gives us $PV = Pmt\left[\frac{(1+r)^1 - (1+r)^{1-n}}{r}\right]$. Then decomposing the fraction, we get $PV = Pmt\left[\frac{1-(1+r)^{1-n}}{r} + \frac{r}{r}\right]$. Finally, simplifying and applying the property $x^{-a} = \frac{1}{x^a}$, we reach our goal:

$$PV = Pmt\frac{1 - \frac{1}{(1+r)^{n-1}}}{r} + 1.$$

TEACHING EXAMPLE 5.3

Principal and Interest Functions

NCTM Content Standards

Numbers and Operations; Algebra

Process Standards

Problem Solving; Reasoning and Proof; Communication; Connections; Representation

Money Applications

Students will

- Review basic arithmetic of mortgages
- Use amortization tables and graphing utilities to determine relationships between interest and principal payments
- Derive detailed mortgage formulas

Discussion and Questions

Ask students, once you have a mortgage, how do you find out the details of it, such as the following:

1. How much will you pay in interest over the life of the mortgage?

2. How are interest and principal paid over time?

3. How much principal will you have left on your mortgage at any point?

Assume for this discussion that a person has a 30-year mortgage of $100,000 at 7% interest, resulting in monthly payments of $665.30.

1. Give them time to do figure this out: How much interest would you pay over the lifetime of the mortgage? The result may astonish them.

> *Answer:* They would pay $139,508 in interest! More than the mortgage principal itself.

Here's how to arrive at the answer. If a person paid $665.30 each month for 30 years, the total payments made would be $239,508 ($665.30 times 12 equals $7,983.60 and multiplying by 30 gives $239,508). So, if a person pays a total of $239,508, and $100,000 is for principal, then the rest must be interest. Voilà, $239,508 minus $100,000 equals $139,508!

2. To see how the interest and principal break down each month, here is an amortization table. It shows the *first 6* and *last 6* months of payments for that $100,000, 30-year mortgage at 7%, discussed in the last teaching example:

Table 5.5 Amortization Table

Month m	Loan Balance $A(m)$	Interest $\frac{0.07}{12} \times A(m)$	Principal $665.30 - \frac{0.07}{12} \times A(m)$	Total Interest $\sum_{i=1}^{360} \left[\frac{0.07}{12} \times A(m) \right]$
1	99,918.03	583.33	81.97	583.33
2	99,835.58	582.86	82.45	1,166.19
3	99,752.66	582.37	82.93	1,748.56
4	99,669.24	581.89	83.41	2,330.45
5	99,585.34	581.40	83.90	2,911.86
6	99,500.96	580.91	84.39	3,492.77
355	3,269.08	22.82	642.49	139,451.47
356	2,622.85	19.07	646.23	139,470.54
357	1,972.85	15.30	650.00	139,485.84
358	1,319.05	11.51	653.79	139,497.35
359	661.44	7.69	657.61	139,505.04
360	0.00	3.86	661.44	139,508.90

The heading spans: "$100,000 at 7% for 30 Years With Monthly Payment = $665.30"

Notice how, at the start, the interest is the lion's share of the monthly payment, but at the end, it is the principal that takes over.

Share a complete amortization table with students (go to www.bankrate.com). Do not give them the expressions that determine interest and principal payments just yet, which appear in the headings in the table above. Rather, have them generate those expressions themselves.

To see this graphically, ask students to use their graphing utility to graph the "interest function," $y_1 = \frac{.07}{12} \times A(m)$, as well as the "principal function," $y_2 = \$665.30 - y_1$, on the same set of axes using a window that covers all 360 months and all possible monthly interest amounts. One such window with accompanying graph is the following:

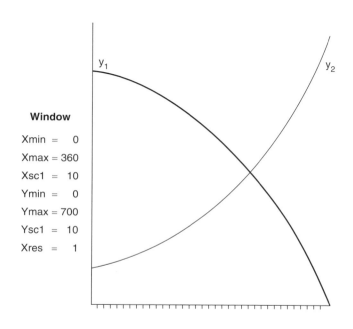

Window

Xmin = 0

Xmax = 360

Xscl = 10

Ymin = 0

Ymax = 700

Yscl = 10

Xres = 1

To be sure they understand the relationship between y_1 and y_2, ask students to describe, without graphing, what the graph of $y_3 = y_1 + y_2$ would look like. They should tell you that it is the horizontal line, as shown below; $y_3 = \$665.30$ because the monthly payment is the sum of interest and principal.

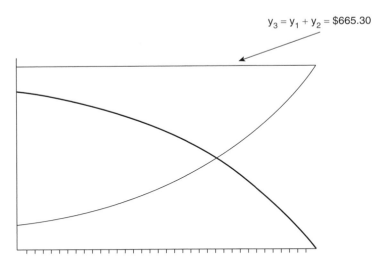

$y_3 = y_1 + y_2 = \$665.30$

Now ask students to use the graph to find the month in which their payment to principal equals their payment to interest. They should tell you that they can find the answer by locating the point of intersection of y_1 and y_2. The coordinates of that point are approximately (241, 333), as shown on the calculator screen as the following:

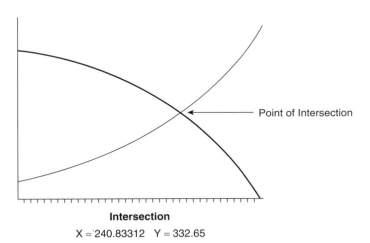

Point of Intersection

Intersection
X = 240.83312   Y = 332.65

Students should tell you that the amounts are about equal during the 241st month, each being about $332.65, which is half of the monthly payment of $665.30. So, for about 240 of 360 months or 2/3 of the life of the mortgage, interest payments exceed principal payments.

3. Finally, how can you determine the amount of principal that is left at any point?

First, let's introduce some new terms and combine them with what we already know.

Let $A(m)$ be the amount we owe on the mortgage in month m, so $A(0)$ would be the total amount that we borrowed, or at time zero. $A(1)$ is then

$$A(1) = A(0) + \text{interest on } A(0) - \text{monthly payment, or}$$
$$= A(0) + r \times A(0) - M,$$

where

$r =$ monthly interest rate
$M =$ monthly mortgage payment

Likewise,

$$A(2) = A(1) + \frac{.07}{12} A(1) - M \text{ and } A(3) = A(2) + \frac{.07}{12} A(2) - M.$$

Continue until students can express this recursive pattern with the formula

$$A(m) = A(m-1) + \frac{.07}{12} A(m-1) - M.$$

Ask them to explain what the formula says in their own words. They should tell you that it means that what we owe this month is what we owed last month plus a month's interest less the monthly payment.

Tell students that the closed form of this formula is

$$A(m) = A(0)(1+r)^m - M[(1+r)^m - 1] \div r$$

and that it can be proven by induction (see extension).

Before we go on, let's use this formula to calculate the monthly payment. We use the fact that at the end of the mortgage, the amount owed is zero, so

$$0 = A(0)(1+r)^m - M[(1+r)^m - 1] \div r,$$

$$M[(1+r)^m - 1] \div r = A(0)(1+r)^m,$$

$$M[(1+r)^m - 1] = A(0)(1+r)^m \times r,$$

$$M = \frac{A(0)(1+r)^m \times r}{(1+r)^m - 1}.$$

In our example,

$$A(0) = \$100,000 \text{ and } r = \frac{.07}{12} \text{ and } m = 360.$$

The monthly payment is then

$$M = \frac{\$100,000 \times \left(1 + \frac{.07}{12}\right)^{360} \times \frac{.07}{12}}{\left(1 + \frac{.07}{12}\right)^{360} - 1} = \$665.30.$$

Now, we use this math to answer our third question: What is the amount of principal remaining at any point in time, or at $A(m)$? We would use this formula:

$$A(m) = A(0)(1+r)^m - Pmt \frac{(1+r)^m - 1}{r}.$$

Let's find the principal remaining after the 100th payment:

$$A(m) = \$100{,}000\left(1 + \frac{.07}{12}\right)^{100} - \$665.30\,\frac{\left(1 + \frac{.07}{12}\right)^{100} - 1}{\frac{.07}{12}},$$

$$A(m) = \$178{,}896 - \$89{,}982,$$

$$A(m) = \$88{,}914.$$

This is the principal remaining after the 100th mortgage payment.

Practice

1. Calculate how much interest you would pay over the life of a 30-year, $175,000 mortgage, at 7.5%; at 6.5%; and at 5.5%.

2. With a graphing utility, find the point of intersection where the interest and principal are equal in a 30-year, $150,000 mortgage, with an interest rate of 8%. Express the answer in the number of months from the start of the mortgage.

3. Determine the remaining principal after the 150th payment in a 30-year, $200,000 mortgage, at 7.5% interest.

Practice Answers

1. $265,370 (using Table 5.4, the monthly payments are $1,223.25. Of those payments, 360 total $440,370. $440,370 minus $175,000 equals $265,370; likewise at 6.5%: $223,160; and at 5.5%: $203,000).

2. The 256th payment.

3. $163,387.

Projects

1. When current mortgage interest rates are 2% below or more than your existing rate, it may be advisable to refinance. Use Table 5.4 to calculate the difference between the interest paid over the life of a 6%, $200,000, 30-year mortgage and an 8%, $200,000, 30-year mortgage. Why do you think you would not refinance for less than a 2% difference?

2. Prove, by induction, that $A(m) = A(0)(1 + r)^m - M\left[(1 + r)^m - 1\right] \div r$ for all $m \in N$.

6

Taxes

How They Work

There are two things certain in life: taxes and changes in taxes.
—Taxpayer

Paying income taxes is an annual ritual of Americans. Understanding how they work can help students not only understand their future responsibility but also understand how to calculate taxes. It is a good opportunity to weave money into a math discussion. There are a number of applications that address the National Council of Teachers of Mathematics (NCTM) standards.

NCTM STANDARDS APPLIED IN THIS CHAPTER

Content

- *Number and Operations.* Understand meanings of operations and how they relate to one another; compute fluently and make reasonable estimates.
- *Algebra.* Understand patterns, relations, and functions; represent and analyze mathematical situations and structures using algebraic symbols; use mathematical models to represent and understand quantitative relationships.

(Continued)

(Continued)

- *Data Analysis and Probability.* Select and use appropriate statistical methods to analyze data.

Process

- Problem Solving; Reasoning and Proof; Communication; Connections; Representation

BACKGROUND: BASICS OF INCOME TAXES—FEDERAL AND STATE

There are a number of different taxes to pay—sales, real estate, estate, FICA—but most of us are most concerned about *income taxes.* On or before April 15, we have to calculate and file our annual 1040 federal tax forms and, for most people, state taxes as well (a few states have no income taxes).

Sales taxes are paid as we buy things, depending on state laws. Some cities tax sales. If you own a house or condo, you pay real estate taxes, which go for local and state government. In most states, this tax is the primary funding for schools. When someone who has a large estate dies, his or her heirs may have to pay estate taxes.

FICA taxes go into Social Security and Medicare programs. FICA stands for Federal Insurance Contributions Act, and in 2006, it was 7.65% of wages up to $94,200. Any higher income is taxed at 1.45%, which is for Medicare only. The amount of $94,200 increases each year (in 2005 it was $90,000). As it turns out, FICA tax can be even more than your income taxes, so it obviously is not to be ignored. Also, if you are self-employed, you have to pay both the employee's and employer's portion, both of which are 7.65%. So, a self-employed person pays a total of 15.3% in FICA taxes.

Income Taxes

It is income tax that gets most of our attention. The problem with this tax, however, besides being a big chunk of money, is that it's complicated. And part of the complication is that there are changes each year. Sometimes the changes are small and sometimes they are big, as was the recent decrease in long-term capital gains and dividends to only 15%. Sometimes there are no changes that affect a taxpayer. Determining the taxes you owe can be very confusing, and that's why the tax-preparation business is booming!

Furthermore, since some transactions are rarely done, they are unfamiliar to us. For instance, if you sell a house or condo, do you know how to calculate the capital gains, if any? (Although this chapter is not meant by any means to be an in-depth guide on taxes, for your information, an individual, in general, gets a $250,000 exemption and a couple gets a $500,000 exemption toward capital gains on a house.)

Let's also state this caveat in bold letters: **This is not a comprehensive guide for taxes** but only a chapter that touches on some basic aspects of taxes that most people should understand. Furthermore, any tax rules mentioned in this chapter are good only at the time of publishing because **taxes can change.** For instance, the 15% tax on dividends and capital gains could change in the future.

The complexity of taxes is appropriately illustrated by the fact that every member of congressional tax committees has someone else do their taxes. Even they do not know all the ins and outs of the tax code. As one tax preparer once said, "The reason that it's called the tax code is because no one can figure it out." Last time we checked, there were about 44,000 pages in this beloved tax code.

Our purpose here is to take some of the mystery out of the basics of federal income taxes (you're on your own with any state income taxes that may apply in your state). So, with some trepidation, here is a chapter on income taxes.

TEACHING EXAMPLE 6.1

Income Tax and FICA

NCTM Content Standards

Numbers and Operations; Algebra

Process Standards

Problem Solving; Connections

Money Applications

Students will

- Calculate taxes from a schedule using percentages
- Calculate taxable income from gross income
- Calculate FICA taxes on gross income
- Calculate marginal and effective tax rates
- Interpret the Laffer curve

Discussion and Questions

Photo by Paul Westbrook.

Tell students that federal income taxes can be approximated from tax schedules:

Table 6.1   Single Federal Tax Rate Schedule for 2006

If Taxable Income Is	The Tax Is
$0 up to $7,750	10%
$7,750 up to $30,650	$755 plus 15% over $7,750
$30,650 up to $74,200	$4,220 plus 25% over $30,650
$74,200 up to $154,800	$15,107 plus 28% over $74,200
$154,800 up to $336,550	$37,675 plus 33% over $154,800
$336,550 and over	$97,653 plus 35% over $336,550

Table 6.2   Married Federal Tax Rate Schedule for 2006

If Taxable Income Is	The Tax Is
$0 up to $15,100	10%
$15,100 up to $61,300	$1,510 plus 15% over $15,100
$61,300 up to $123,700	$8,440 plus 25% over $61,300
$123,700 up to $188,450	$24,040 plus 28% over $123,700
$188,450 up to $336,550	$42,170 plus 33% over $188,450
$336,550 and over	$91,043 plus 35% over $336,550

These schedules allow you to see the federal income tax brackets so you can gain some understanding of how taxes are calculated.

Ask the students to use the tax schedules for 2006 (shown just above) to calculate the amount of federal income taxes a single person would owe if he or she earned $30,000.

(Although we'll make this more complicated in a minute with standard deductions and exemptions, just have the students use the schedule.)

By examining the schedules, there are two tax brackets we need to use: the 10% and 15% brackets. If we earned more than $30,650, we would have to use the third bracket as well.

The simplest way to calculate the taxes would be to go to the line that has the highest bracket that applies—in this case, the second bracket:

$7,550 up to $30,650 → $755 plus 15% over $7,550

As you will note, the $755 is the calculated tax on the first $7,550 (10% of $7,550 is $755).

So, we have to calculate how much we have to pay over $7,550 up to our earnings of $30,000. The amount of our income above $7,550 is $22,450 ($30,000 minus $7,550 is $22,450).

That $22,450 is all taxed at 15%, which is $3,367.50.

Now add the amount of taxes for both the 10% and 15% brackets to get the total of $4,122.50 ($755 plus $3,367.50 is $4,122.50). We are able to round, so, if your taxable income were $30,000, you would pay $4,122 even.

Now we want to add our first level of complexity, but this is helpful because it reduces your taxes.

Each person is given a deduction and an exemption, as follows:

Federal Tax Deductions and Exemptions for 2006

Standard Deductions:

Single: $5,150
Married: $10,300

Exemptions:

Per person: $3,300

So, if a single person earned a gross income of $35,000, his or her taxable income would be only $26,550 ($35,000 minus $5,150 minus $3,300 equals $26,550).

You can "itemize" deductions, but unless you have a mortgage and pay real estate taxes, the standard deduction is usually the higher deduction amount.

You are also required to pay FICA or Social Security and Medicare taxes on income. This is deducted automatically from your paycheck. This totals 7.65% of your pay, up to $94,200 in 2006. (It increases each year.)

Thus, if a single person earned a gross salary of $35,000, there would be $2,677.50 to be paid in FICA taxes, besides income taxes. A person who earned $50,000 would have to pay $3,825 in FICA taxes, besides income taxes.

Finally, two terms are used in taxes to express how much is being taxed: the marginal tax rate and the effective tax rate.

- The marginal tax rate is the highest tax bracket in which a person is taxed.
- The effective tax rate is the average tax being assessed.

As an example of a marginal tax rate—in the case of a single person who is earning a taxable amount of $30,000—the marginal tax rate is 15% because that is the highest tax bracket used for the calculation. The usefulness of this is to know what the tax would be if the person earned more money. The next dollar would be taxed at 15%. If the earnings would be much more, then, obviously, the person would slip into the next bracket, or 25%. Then the next dollar would be taxed at that higher bracket, or at 25%.

As an example of an effective tax rate—in the case of a single person who is earning a gross amount of $30,000 (taxable amount of $22,450)—the tax is calculated for this individual as $4,122. This is 13.7% of the total income of $30,000 ($4,122 divided by $30,000 equals .137 or 13.7%). This is the effective tax rate. It shows the overall average percent of how much the person is paying in income taxes relative to the gross earnings.

Practice

1. Calculate the federal income taxes for a single person who earned a gross income of $35,000 and took the standard deduction and one exemption.

2. Calculate the FICA tax for a single person who earned a gross income of $35,000.

3. Calculate the combined amount of federal income taxes and FICA taxes for a married couple (with only one person working) who earned a gross income of $50,000 and took the standard deduction and 2 exemptions.

4. Using the results in Question 3, what are the marginal and effective income tax rates of this couple?

5. Suppose a married couple files their federal income taxes for 2006 and has a taxable income of $63,000:
   a. How much would they pay in federal income taxes according to the 2006 tax schedule?
   b. How much would they pay if they put $400 a month (for a total of $4,800) into an IRA, 401(k), or 403(b), all tax-deductible accounts?

Practice Answers

1. $3,605. Given the taxable income of $26,550, calculated above, the tax is calculated by first subtracting $7,550 from $26,550 to get the amount in the 15% bracket, which is $19,000. That tax is $2,850 ($19,000 times .15 [15%] equals $2,850). That is added to $755 for the first bracket, and the answer of $3,605 is obtained ($2,850 plus $755 equals $3,605).

2. $2,677.50 ($35,000 times .0765 [7.65%] equals $2,677.50).

3. $8,035. To find the taxable income, subtract the standard deduction of $10,300 and 2 exemptions of $6,600 to determine the taxable income, or $33,100 ($50,000 minus $10,300 minus $6,600 equals $33,100). To find the tax on $33,100, go to Table 6.2 and find the bracket where the highest amount is taxed, or the second bracket taxed as 15%. $18,000 is the amount over $15,100 and thus is taxed at 15% and is $2,700 ($33,100 minus $15,100 equals $18,000), and this is added to $1,510 from the first bracket for a total tax of $4,210 ($2,700 plus $1,510 equals $4,210).

   To find the FICA taxes, multiply the gross of $50,000 by 7.65% to obtain $3,825 ($50,000 times .0765 [7.65%] equals $3,825).

   Finally, the total of the two taxes is $8,025 ($4,210 plus $3,825 equals $8,035).

4. 15% and 8.42%. To find the marginal tax rate, determine the highest tax bracket, which is 15%. The effective tax rate of the income tax is $4,210 divided by $50,000, which equals 8.42% ($4,210 divided by $50,000 equals .0842 or 8.42%). This does not include the FICA taxes.

5. $8,865 and $7,975.
   a. $8,440 + .25($63,000 − $61,300) = $8,865.
   b. $63,000 − $4,800 = $58,200 and then $1,510 + .15($58,200 − $15,100) = $7,975.

Extension

The Laffer curve has been promoted by economist Arthur Laffer to justify tax cuts. The curve is parabolic and looks like the following:

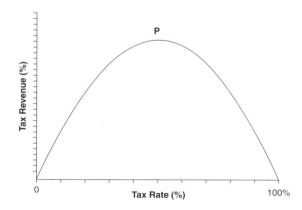

Find out what the significance of the vertex and x-intercepts of this curve is as related to taxes. Also, report on the political controversy associated with this seemingly harmless parabola.

TEACHING EXAMPLE 6.2

Capital Gains and Losses

NCTM Content Standards

Numbers and Operations

Process Standards

Problem Solving; Connections

Money Applications

Students will

- Identify the category of capital gains or losses
- Combine capital gains and losses to determine the net gains or losses
- Calculate the appropriate tax on capital gains or losses

Discussion and Questions

Explain to your students that capital gains taxes are paid if you make money on an investment, and capital losses are allowed if you lose money on an investment. These investments are typically mutual funds or individual stocks or bonds.

Importantly, there are various rules to follow when calculating the gains and losses and the actual taxes to be paid. We are using only the simple rules for instructional purposes. Capital gains and losses, depending on the situation as well as the actual asset, may be much more complex than we are explaining here.

A gain or loss is calculated only when an investment has actually been sold. We are not talking about a paper gain or loss—that is, what your investments are worth at any point in time, which can fluctuate from day to day.

There are four categories of capital gains and losses:

1. Long-term capital gain, which is an investment held a year plus a day or more, is currently taxed at 15%.

2. Long-term capital loss is an investment held a year plus a day or more, and up to $3,000 is allowed yearly for taxes.

3. Short-term gain, which is an investment held for a year or less, is taxed at regular income tax rates.

4. Short-term loss, which is an investment held for a year or less, is deducted from regular income before taxes are determined.

If a taxpayer has capital gains and losses in several categories, there is a "netting" process, which results in the following rule:

Net Your Longs, Net Your Shorts, and Then Net Your Nets

In other words, a taxpayer has to calculate the resultant gain or loss and then pay the appropriate tax or take the appropriate loss.

Here's an example:

A taxpayer has the following transactions to report:

$2,000 long-term gain
$1,500 long-term loss
$750 short-term gain
$1,200 short-term loss

Question: What is the resultant "netting"?
Answer: $50 long-term gain, taxed at 15%.

First: To find the long-term nets, subtract the gain and loss against each other, with the result in this case being a $500 long-term gain ($2,000 minus $1,500 equals $500).

Second: To find the short-term nets, subtract the gain and loss against each other, with the result in this case being a $450 short-term loss.

Third: To find the net of both, subtract the gain and loss against each other, with the result in this case being a $50 long-term gain, which is taxed at 15%.

If there are long-term and short-term gains, then each is taxed accordingly. That is, a long-term gain is taxed at 15%, and a short-term gain is taxed at regular income tax rates.

If there are long-term and short-term losses, then only a maximum of $3,000 can be deducted each year.

Practice

1. Find the resultant gain or loss of the following capital gains and losses: A taxpayer has the following transactions to report:

   - $3,000 long-term gain
   - $500 long-term loss
   - $2,590 short-term gain
   - $1,050 short-term loss

2. Find the resultant gain or loss of the following capital gains and losses: A taxpayer has the following transactions to report:

   - $2,000 long-term gain
   - $800 long-term loss
   - $350 short-term gain
   - $950 short-term loss

Practice Answers

1. $2,500 long-term gain taxed at 15% and $1,540 short-term gain taxed at regular income tax rates.

2. $600 long-term gain, taxed at 15%.

TEACHING EXAMPLE 6.3

How Uncle Sam Uses Tax Dollars

NCTM Content Standards

Numbers and Operations; Data Analysis; Probability

Process Standards

Problem Solving; Reasoning and Proof; Communication; Connections; Representation

Money Applications

Students will

- Using pie chart percentages, calculate equivalent dollar amounts
- Using dollar amounts, compare different categories

Discussion and Questions

Ask the students to examine the following two pie charts, which were included in the tax booklet from the Internal Revenue Service (IRS). They are from 2004:

Figure 6.1   Major Categories of Federal Income and Outlays for 2004

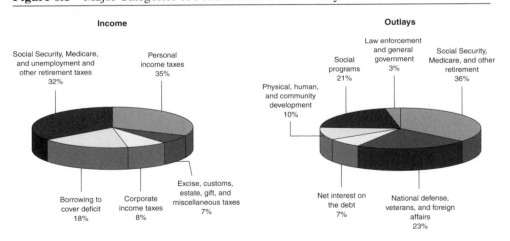

For 2004, federal income was $1.9 trillion, and the federal outlays were $2.3 trillion. Tell students that if outlay is greater than income, there is a deficit. Ask students to

- Determine the 2004 deficit in billions of dollars
- Justify their answer

Correct responses are as follows:

- The deficit for 2004 was $400 billion.
- Subtract income from outlay by using the distributive law, then convert to billions by using the associative law:

$$\$2.3 \times 10^{12} - \$1.9 \times 10^{12} = (\$2.3 - \$1.9) \times 10^{12} = \$0.4 \times 10^{12}$$
$$0.4 \times 10^{12} - (\$0.4 \times 10^{3} \times 10^{9}) = \$400 \times 10^{9} = \$400,000,000,000.$$

Now ask students to

- Calculate the actual dollar amount of income from personal income taxes for 2004
- Explain their work

Correct responses are as follows:

- $665 billion
- Personal income taxes were 35% of federal income, which was $1.9 trillion:

$$0.35(\$1.9 \times 10^{12}) = \$0.665 \times 10^{12} = \$665 \times 10^{9} = \$665,000,000,000.$$

Finally, ask students to

- Calculate the actual dollar amount of outlays for Social Security, Medicare, and other retirement programs
- Explain their work

Correct responses are as follows:

- $828 billion
- Social Security, Medicare, and other federal retirement programs were 36% of the federal outlay, which was $2.3 trillion:

$$\$0.36(\$2.3 \times 10^{12}) = \$0.828 \times 10^{12} = \$828 \times 10^{9} = \$828,000,000,000.$$

Practice

1. In 2004, what was the difference between income and outlay for Social Security, Medicare, and other retirement programs?

2. In 2004, what is the dollar amount of net interest on U.S. debt?

Practice Answers

1. $163 billion. First, calculate the dollar amount of 35% of the income or $665 billion ($1,900 billion times .35 [35%] equals $665). Second, calculate the dollar amount of 36% of the outlays or $828 billion ($2,300 billion times .36 [36%] equals $828 billion). Third, find the difference or $163 billion ($828 billion minus $665 billion equals $163 billion).

2. $161 billion ($2,300 billion times .07 [7%] equals $161 billion).

Extension

There are some big differences between the 2004 (see Figure 6.1) and 1999 (see Figure 6.2) federal income and outlays. Contrast and compare them, giving some of the conditions in the country at these times that contributed to the differences.

Figure 6.2   Major Categories of Federal Income and Outlays for Fiscal Year 1999

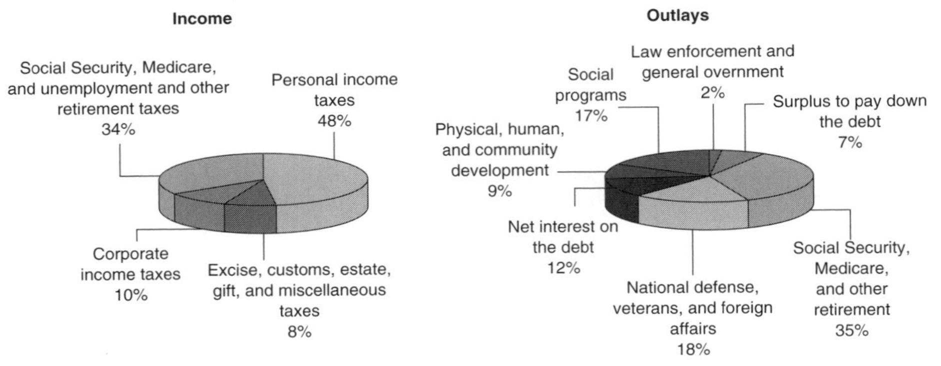

Income

Social Security, Medicare, and unemployment and other retirement taxes
34%

Personal income taxes
48%

Corporate income taxes
10%

Excise, customs, estate, gift, and miscellaneous taxes
8%

Outlays

Social programs
17%

Physical, human, and community development
9%

Law enforcement and general overnment
2%

Surplus to pay down the debt
7%

Net interest on the debt
12%

National defense, veterans, and foreign affairs
18%

Social Security, Medicare, and other retirement
35%

SOURCE: Internal Revenue Service (www.irs.gov).

Economics

Supply and Demand, Inflation, and the GDP

Everybody talks about it, but doesn't do anything about it. It's not the weather—it's the economy!

—Anonymous

U nderstanding the basics of the economy not only can help students appreciate the reality of work, jobs, and income, but it also can help them understand how the overall economy works. It also is a very good way to weave math into the discussion. There are a number of applications that address the National Council of Teachers of Mathematics (NCTM) standards.

NCTM STANDARDS APPLIED IN THIS CHAPTER

Content

- *Number and Operations.* Understand meanings of operations and how they relate to one another; compute fluently and make reasonable estimates.
- *Algebra.* Understand patterns, relations, and functions; represent and analyze mathematical situations and structures using algebraic symbols; use mathematical models to represent and understand quantitative relationships.
- *Geometry.* Apply transformations to analyze mathematical situations.

Process

- Problem Solving; Reasoning and Proof; Communication; Connections; Representation

BACKGROUND: ECONOMICS, SUPPLY AND DEMAND, INFLATION, AND THE GDP

It's sometimes called the "dismal science" because it can be dry and difficult to understand. But what could be dry about the basis of our economy, which drives our individual financial health? Three basic subjects are mentioned in this chapter: supply and demand, inflation, and GDP (gross domestic product). All potentially dry, but very important.

Supply and demand is a basic truth of life. If the price for something you want decreases, you are more apt to buy it, such as wide-screen TVs. Inflation is also an important topic because it tells us how much more we have to pay for our lifestyle. It is measured by the CPI (consumer price index).

GDP is perhaps the one single figure that summarizes how well our economy is doing, overall. It is the total of all the goods and services produced within the United States, measured each quarter. It is given in "real" terms, meaning that the amount of inflation has already been subtracted out. For instance, for all of 2005, our GDP was reported as 3.5%, with inflation at 3.4%.

But to understand this GDP figure in more depth, the actual numerical increase in GDP for 2005, or "raw" number, was 6.9%. This is technically called the "nominal" GDP. But that's not reported to the public because it's misleading. Inflation needs to be subtracted out. By subtracting 3.4% inflation out of 6.9%, the resultant or "real" GDP is 3.5% (6.9% minus 3.4% equals 3.5%).

Here's a way to understand why this is done. If, in a particular year, the GDP actually increased "nominally" by 3%, but inflation at the same time increased by 3%, would the economy have grown? No, because the 3% increase in GDP was due to inflation. The amount of goods and services would have increased only because of increased prices. Thus, we see only the "real" GDP, the amount that the economy actually grew, after inflation.

TEACHING EXAMPLE 7.1

Supply and Demand Functions

NCTM Content Standards

Numbers and Operations; Algebra; Geometry

Process Standards

Problem Solving; Reasoning and Proof; Communication; Connections; Representation

Money Applications

Students will

- Interpret graphs
- Transform lines
- Calculate from an index

Discussion and Questions

Engage students by asking them to give examples of something they

- Were interested in buying but did not buy until the price came down (examples: computers, iPod, and shoes!)
- Would buy no matter what the price (examples: soda, CDs, and shoes!)

Tell students that these questions have to do with the most basic law in economics: supply and demand. It is a law that plays into life in many ways. This law is usually illustrated by two curves: one showing the demand, which represents what you as a consumer will do, and one showing the

Photo by Paul Westbrook.

supply, which represents what a company will do. While the two curves sometimes are shown as curved lines, they are as frequently shown as straight lines, as follows:

Supply and Demand Curves

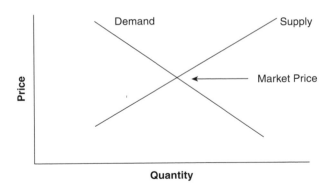

The basic economic concept behind supply and demand is that the price of a product determines whether you will buy it or in what quantity you will buy it. In general, the lower the price, the more likely that you will buy it because you can afford it. This is the *demand*.

The higher the price, however, the more likely the producer will produce more of it because it will make more money. This is the *supply*. The price that is just right balances the supply and demand curves and is called the market price or the *price equilibrium*. It is the *y*-value at the point where the two curves meet.

The demand is said to be *elastic* if the demand changes when the price changes. That is, if the price is decreased, then more people buy the product. It's cheaper. It's called elastic because it stretches.

If, however, the demand stays relatively the same as the price increases or decreases, then it is said that the demand is *inelastic*. For example, when the "Tickle-Me Elmo" doll was at the height of its fad, it sold no matter the price. That's an example of inelasticity.

Supply is likewise elastic and inelastic. Companies may continue to produce a product even though its price is declining, say, because there are more producers in the market. However, after a point, a company may simply stop producing the product because it can no longer make a profit.

To sum: Demand is the quantity that consumers are willing to buy at a given price, and supply is the quantity that producers are willing to sell at a given price. Where these two forces meet is the market price for that product or service. Said another way, the lower the price, the more consumers are willing to buy. The higher the price, the more producers are willing to produce.

For example, have students consider the following situation:

Suppose that you are thinking about buying a bottle of water because you think that it is better for you than tap water and because you can carry it with you. Given these considerations, at what price are you willing to buy a bottle of water?

The current price at many convenience stores is $1.00. What if the price increases to $1.25? Would you stop buying it and find an alternative, say, of buying an empty bottle and filling it at work or school? What if the price went to

$1.50? At some point, you probably stop buying bottled water and find an alternative. This is "demand" in action.

Consider the following hypothetical table of sales of bottled water at a local convenience store:

Quantity of Bottles Demanded	Quantity of Bottles Supplied	Price per Bottle
100	220	130 ¢
120	200	120 ¢
140	180	110 ¢
160	160	100 ¢
180	140	90 ¢
200	120	80 ¢

The store manager knows that customers will probably buy more if the prices are lower, but the manager wants to have a reasonable profit margin. Likewise, the manager doesn't want to drive people away with prices that are too high. The manager wants our help in determining the "market" price.

Ask students to help the manager out by

- Finding the equations of the supply and demand lines
- Graphing the equations
- Identifying the point of intersection in order to identify the market price

Their results should be as follows:

- Demand equation: $y = -0.5x + 180$
- Supply equation: $y = 0.5x + 20$

(Students should use the data in the table above and slope-intercept or point-slope form to find the equation.)

- A graph should look like the following:

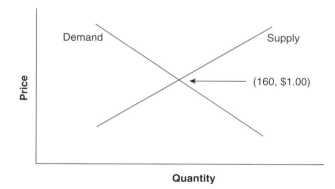

- The point of intersection is (160, $1.00). So, the price the manager should charge is $1.00. (Students can get the intersection from their graphing calculators or solve the system of equations $y = -0.5x + 180$ and $y = 0.5x + 20$ algebraically.)

But the demand and supply lines are not static. They are good for only a limited period of time since things can and do change.

For instance, let's say that there was a local flood that caused a heightened concern about the quality of tap water in the area. Suppose this could cause an increase of 100 bottles in demand at every price level. We can use a translation of the demand curve to illustrate this on our supply and demand curve as follows:

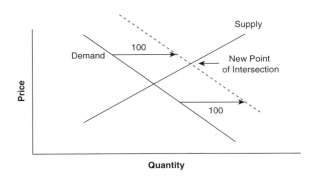

The demand line has been translated 100 units to the right since demand has increased. The supply curve remains the same. Obviously, the manager has noticed this increase in demand and has accordingly decided to increase the price but, once again, needs to know what to charge. Let's help the manager once more by doing the following:

- Finding the equation of the new demand line
- Identifying the new point of intersection in order to identify the new "market" price

Their results should be the following:

- New demand equation: $y = -0.5(x - 100) + 180$ or simply $y = -0.5x + 230$

To express a translation of a units horizontally and b units vertically, we replace x with $x - a$ and y with $y - b$. Since there was no vertical translation, $y = -0.5 + 180$ becomes $y = -0.5(x - 100) + 180$.

The new point of intersection is (210, $1.25). So, the price the manager should now charge is $1.25 per bottle. (Students can get the intersection from their graphing calculators or solve the system of equations $y = -0.5x + 230$ and $y = 0.5x + 20$ algebraically.)

This is supply and demand in action. Since the customers want more, they will probably be willing to pay more for it. Thus, the point at which the two lines meet is now higher in the graph. The price has been adjusted, which demonstrates the market forces in play.

Now, let's create a different situation. Let's say instead of having a local flood that causes an increase in demand, another convenience store opens for business a few blocks away. Now there is more supply in the community. What happens to our graph?

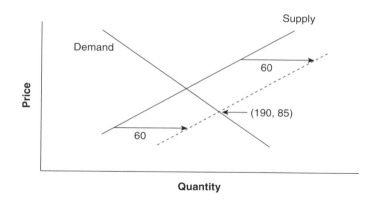

Because there is more competition (supply), the supply increases, so the supply line now moves to the right. In the spirit of competition, the new store decreases its price to draw customers. Soon the older store also decreases its prices to match the new store. The marketplace often works this way. The graph thus shows how moving the supply line to the right results, in general, in a decrease in the market price.

Ask the students to examine the graph and answer the following questions:

- How far did the supply line move to the right?
- What is its new equation?
- What is the new market value?

Their results should be the following:

- The supply line moved 60 units to the right since, at the point of intersection, $0.5(x - a) + 20 = 0.5x - 10$. Solving for a, we get $a = 60$.
- The new equation is $y = 0.5(x - 60) + 20$ or, simply, $y = 0.5x - 10$.
- The new market value is the y-value at the point of intersection, 85¢.

Practice

1. If the price of a product or service *increases*, what generally happens to the quantity of the products *purchased* by consumers, or the demand curve?

2. If the price of a product or service *increases*, what generally happens to the quantity of products *produced* by companies, or the supply curve?

3. If the price of a product or service *decreases*, what generally happens to the quantity of a product or service *purchased* by consumers, or the demand curve?

4. If the price of a product or service *decreases*, what generally happens to the quantity of products *produced* by companies, or the supply curve?

5. Calculate the revenue from sales based on the table of values in this chapter. Explain why you sometimes used the value for demand and sometimes for supply to determine that revenue.

Practice Answers

1. Quantity decreases, or you tend to buy less.

2. Quantity increases, or companies tend to make more.

3. Quantity increases, or you tend to buy more.

4. Quantity decreases, or companies tend to make less.

5. Demand is used when it is less than the supply, and supply is used when it is less than demand.

Bottles Demanded	Bottles Supplied	Price per Bottle	Sales Revenue
100	220	$1.30	$100 \times \$1.30 = \$130$
120	200	$1.20	$120 \times \$1.20 = \$144$
140	180	$1.10	$140 \times \$1.10 = \$154$
160	160	$1.00	$160 \times \$1.00 = \$160$
180	140	$0.90	$140 \times \$0.90 = \$126$
200	120	$0.80	$120 \times \$0.80 = \$96$

TEACHING EXAMPLE 7.2

Inflation and the GDP

NCTM Content Standards

Numbers and Operations

Process Standards

Problem Solving; Connections

Money Applications

Students will

- Analyze a table
- Interpret values from a table
- Calculate values from an index

Discussion and Questions

Two of the most important economic measurements are inflation and GDP.

Inflation measures how much the overall prices have increased. People at the Bureau of Labor Statistics (www.bls.gov) go to actual stores and measure the prices of goods and services. This information is called the CPI. These prices are reported each month. During a year, some prices will increase, some will remain the same, and some prices will actually decrease.

The bureau also has determined what is in the average "basket of goods and services" an average person uses. It adds up the prices of these items at one point in time and compares it to another point in time. It creates indices (or indexes) and then calculates the amounts of increases in terms of percentages. Here is a listing of the annual price indices from 1996 through 2005:

Table 7.1   End-of-Year Inflation Index

1996	158.6
1997	161.3
1998	163.9
1999	168.3
2000	174.0
2001	176.7
2002	180.9
2003	184.3
2004	190.3
2005	196.8

To determine the percentage from these index values, a simple percentage is calculated. For instance, the increase for 2005, over 2004, is 3.4%.

This is calculated by subtracting the difference between 2005 and 2004, which is 6.5 (196.8 minus 190.3 equals 6.5). Then 6.5 is divided by the starting value of 190.3 to obtain the amount of increase that occurred by percentage, or in this case, 3.4% (6.5 divided by 190.3 equals .034, or 3.4%).

Practice

Calculate the percentage increases for each year, from 1997 through 2005, from the yearly indices.

Practice Answers

1997: 1.7% (161.3 minus 158.6 equals 2.7; 2.7 divided by 158.6 equals .0170, or 1.7%).

1998: 1.6% (163.9 minus 161.3 equals 2.6; 2.6 divided by 161.3 equals .0161, or 1.6%).

1999: 2.7% (168.3 minus 163.9 equals 4.4; 4.4 divided by 163.9 equals .0268, or 2.7%).

2000: 3.4% (174.0 minus 168.3 equals 5.7; 5.7 divided by 168.3 equals .0338, or 3.4%).

2001: 1.6% (176.7 minus 174.0 equals 2.7; 2.7 divided by 174 equals .0155, or 1.6%).

2002: 2.4% (180.9 minus 176.7 equals 4.2; 4.2 divided by 176.7 equals .0237, or 2.4%).

2003: 1.9% (184.3 minus 180.9 equals 3.4; 3.4 divided by 180.9 equals .0187, or 1.9%).

2004: 3.3% (190.3 minus 184.3 equals 6; 6 divided by 184.3 equals .0325, or 3.3%).

2005: 3.4% (196.8 minus 190.3 equals 6.5; 6.5 divided by 190.3 equals .034, or 3.4%).

GDP or gross domestic product is the total dollar value of all the goods and services produced in our country. It is reported each month by the Bureau of Economic Analysis (www.bea.gov). Before it is reported, however, the amount of inflation has been subtracted out. Here is a listing of the annual GDP for a recent 10-year period:

Table 7.2   Yearly GDP

1997	4.5%
1998	4.2%
1999	4.5%
2000	3.7%
2001	(0.8%)
2002	1.6%
2003	2.7%
2004	4.2%
2005	3.5%

If the amount of inflation in 1997 was 1.7%, then the actual GDP was 6.2%. This is called "nominal" GDP. However, since it's misleading, the amount of inflation for the year is subtracted out to get the "real" GDP (6.2% minus 1.7% equals 4.5%).

Practice

Calculate the actual, or "nominal," increases of GDP for 1997 through 2005.

Practice Answers
Nominal GDP

1997: 6.2% (4.5% plus 1.7% equals 6.2%).
1998: 5.8% (4.2% plus 1.6% equals 5.8%).
1999: 7.2% (4.5% plus 2.7% equals 7.2%).
2000: 7.1% (3.7% plus 3.4% equals 7.1%).
2001: 0.8% (−0.8% plus 1.6% equals 0.8%).
2002: 4.0% (1.6% plus 2.4% equals 4.0%).
2003: 4.6% (2.7% plus 1.9% equals 4.6%).
2004: 7.5% (4.2% plus 3.3% equals 7.5%).
2005: 6.9% (3.5% plus 3.4% equals 6.9%).

Extension

Have students go to www.bls.gov (Bureau of Labor Statistics) and www.bea.gov (Bureau of Economic Analysis) for economic information.

1. Have them find the information used in this Teaching Activity.

2. Have them find other information on these sites and report on one statistic.

8

In Business for Yourself

Business Plan and Break-Even Analysis

Business is the engine that produces wealth.

—Anonymous

Not everyone will work for someone else; some will start or buy into a business. As such, having some understanding of the financial basics of running a company can help students appreciate the difficulty and the rewards of self-employment. It also is a very good way to weave math into the discussion. There are a number of applications that address the National Council of Teachers of Mathematics (NCTM) standards.

NCTM STANDARDS APPLIED IN THIS CHAPTER

Content

- *Number and Operations*. Understand meanings of operations and how they relate to one another; compute fluently and make reasonable estimates.

(Continued)

(Continued)

- *Algebra.* Understand patterns, relations, and functions; represent and analyze mathematical situations and structures using algebraic symbols; use mathematical models to represent and understand quantitative relationships.

Process

- Problem Solving; Reasoning and Proof; Communication; Connections; Representation

BACKGROUND: IN BUSINESS FOR YOURSELF— A BUSINESS PLAN AND BREAK-EVEN ANALYSIS

Having a business of your own is often romanticized. It sounds great. You're the boss. However, your workday is typically longer than it would be if you worked for someone else, especially when you get started—all responsibility is yours. In addition, the Small Business Administration estimates that only 66% of small businesses survive 2 years, and only 44% survive 4 years.

The rewards are there, however, if you succeed. Yes, you are your own boss, so to speak. It usually is said that you have personal freedom, but that really is tempered by reality: Your customers are your boss! So, everyone has a boss, whether we recognize it or not.

We cover two critical aspects of starting a business in this chapter. First, we review a pro forma income statement, which is a "must do" to get started. *Pro forma* simply means a projected financial statement. Second, we review break-even analysis. It's usually in the form of a diagram that shows, through income and expenses, at what point you start making money. That is, of course, the most critical point for a business.

A pro forma statement is a best guess of what a business will perform, usually for the next 3 years. Although there are other important financial statements, we will concentrate in this chapter on the income statement. Others are the balance sheet, which shows assets and liabilities, and the cash flow statement, which shows projected cash income.

A business plan is more than a pro forma income and expense projection; it is a complete statement and commentary of the what, why, and how your business will proceed and how you expect to make a profit. It begins with a detailed description of your product or service. It includes your rationale for offering the product or service, a marketing plan, how you will finance your business, and how many people you need to hire. It also includes research on similar businesses in the area and the potential for attracting enough customers for an ongoing business. A complete business plan is required if you want to get financing for your business through your local bank.

This chapter uses an example of a business that students can relate to, a bicycle shop. We assume the individual has little money for the business, so it begins as a part-time activity while holding another job. Thus, the individual will start with a repair shop just in the evenings. The individual then hopes, after establishing a reputation for good repairs, to expand to a modest store where more repairs can be made and a small line of bicycles can be sold. Finally, the individual hopes to move to a larger store in a good location with an active repair shop and selling a full line of bicycles.

Some terminology is in order as we look at business income statements from top to bottom. The total income for a company can be variously called revenue, sales, or income. For retail companies, the cost of goods sold is the cost of buying their goods at wholesale. When the cost of goods sold is subtracted from income, the result can be called gross profit or gross margin. Additional costs such as advertising, rent, and employee costs are then subtracted from gross profit, and the result is called operating profit or operating margin. When there are other costs to be subtracted, then the bottom line is determined and is variously called profit, net profit, net income, or net earnings.

A break-even analysis is a graphic display with important relationships of income and expenses, given different amounts of output. This is typically used for a manufacturing business. Fixed costs are normally the costs of rent, lights, and other costs, whether any products are produced or not. Variable costs are those costs of material and employees once production has begun. Total costs are the sum of variable and fixed costs.

The break-even point is reached when the revenues equal the total costs. It is a very important point because thereafter, as more products are made, there is a profit. Although straight lines are used in our examples, in many cases, businesses determine that their actual revenues and expenses are best represented by curved lines.

TEACHING EXAMPLE 8.1

Starting a Business: Pro Forma Income Statement

NCTM Content Standards

Numbers and Operations

Process Standards

Problem Solving; Connections

Money Applications

Students will

- Analyze tables
- Calculate and compare percents

Discussion and Questions

Rhoda Bike would like to start a bicycle repair business. This, at first, is intended to start as an evening business, while she holds down a regular job. Rhoda will simply rent a local garage and advertise for repairs. She hopes to attract enough activity that could be the basis of a full-time business.

If Rhoda can get enough customers, a modest shop will be opened. At that point, Rhoda hopes to rent a storefront so more repairs can be done and she will have room to sell a limited number of bicycles. Finally, if all goes well, she hopes to open a larger store in a good location offering a complete repair shop and a full line of bicycles.

Ask the students to examine the projected income and expenses of this startup business and answer the questions below the pro forma income statement:

Photo by Paul Westbrook.

Table 8.1 Pro Forma Income Statement for a Bicycle Shop

	2007	2008	2009
Income	$15,000	$30,000	$75,000
Costs of Goods Sold	$1,500	$8,000	$25,000
Gross Profit	$13,500	$22,000	$50,000
Advertising	$2,000	$3,000	$10,000
Rent	$3,600	$7,000	$7,500
Profit	$7,900	$12,000	$32,500

Tell the students that "costs of goods sold" means the costs of materials that have to be bought for repairing bikes. For instance, if replacement tires are needed, then it is the cost of those tires. It would also include the costs of any repair tools Rhoda has to buy to perform repairs.

Also tell the students that in 2007, the pro forma reflects that Rhoda is planning to start and work out of a rented garage. In 2008 and 2009, Rhoda is planning to rent a small shop where a limited number of bikes can be offered for sale besides allowing for a larger repair area.

Also tell the students that Rhoda is hopeful that in 2010, the business will move into a larger store in a prime traffic area with a full line of bikes to be sold, besides an expanded repair area.

Also, the profits, or the "bottom line," represent Rhoda's salary.

Ask the students: Has the percent of costs of goods sold in 2008 and 2009 increased or decreased relative to income in 2007?

Answer: Increased. As shown in the following table, the percent increased from 10% in 2007 to 27% and 33% the next 2 years, respectively.

	2007	2008	2009
Income	$15,000	$30,000	$75,000
Costs of Goods Sold	$1,500	$8,000	$25,000
Percent	10	27	33

Ask the students: Has the percent of profit in 2008 and 2009 increased or decreased relative to income in 2007?

Answer: Decreased then slightly increased. As shown in the following table, the percent decreased from 53% in 2007, to 40% in 2008, and then to 43% the next year.

	2007	2008	2009
Income	$15,000	$30,000	$75,000
Profit	$7,900	$12,000	$32,500
Percent	53	40	43

Practice

1. Calculate if advertising costs have increased or decreased relative to income from 2007 to 2008 and 2009.

2. Calculate if advertising costs have increased or decreased relative to costs of goods sold from 2007 to 2008 and 2009.

3. Calculate if the profit has increased or decreased relative to income from 2007 to 2008 and 2009.

Practice Answers

1. The percent has remained about the same.

	2007	2008	2009
Income	$15,000	$30,000	$75,000
Advertising	$2,000	$3,000	$10,000
Percent	13	10	13

2. The percent has decreased significantly from 2007.

	2007	2008	2009
Costs of Goods Sold	$1,500	$8,000	$25,000
Advertising	$2,000	$3,000	$10,000
Percent	133	38	40

3. The percent has decreased slightly from 2007.

	2007	2008	2009
Income	$15,000	$30,000	$75,000
Profit	$7,900	$12,000	$32,500
Percent	49	40	43

Possible Project

Have the students think about a business they might start and write a one-page paper that describes the following: what the product or service is, why you think it could be a success, and what marketing would be necessary. Then have them prepare a pro forma for 3 years. Finally, have them calculate the various percent comparisons, as above, and explain the numbers.

TEACHING EXAMPLE 8.2

Revenue, Costs, and Break-Even Points

NCTM Content Standards

Numbers and Operations; Algebra

Process Standards

Problem Solving; Reasoning and Proof; Communication; Connections; Representation

Money Applications

Students will

- Read a break-even graph
- Interpret points and slope in the context of business
- Find equations of revenue and cost lines to determine the break-even point

Discussion and Questions

Tell students that one of the most critical calculations that someone starting his or her own business must do is to determine when the revenue from sales will cover his or her costs of doing business. The point at which this occurs is called the break-even point for that business.

A break-even analysis shows at what point a profit can begin to be earned. It usually is used for a startup business, but it can also be used when a company wants to improve its profits. It is a graphic display showing the various incomes and costs, given amounts of output.

Here is an example of a break-even analysis:

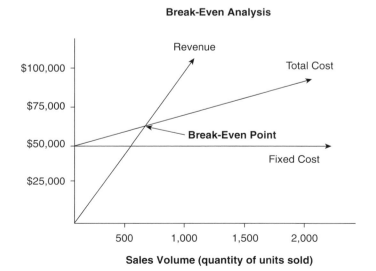

Break-Even Analysis

Tell students that *fixed costs* are the basic costs of maintaining a store or factory even if no products are made and sold.

Ask students the following:

- What the graph says about fixed costs
- Find the equation of the fixed cost line

Correct responses are as follows:

- The graph tells us that no matter how many products are sold, fixed costs will always be $50,000. That is why the graph shows a horizontal line.
- The equation is $y = 50,000$.

Tell students that *variable costs* are those costs that increase as production increases, such as costs of materials and employees. The variable costs are usually directly related to sales, so when sales increase, so do the variable costs.

Ask students to do the following:

- Find the variable cost per unit if the variable cost for producing 1,500 units is $25,000

Correct response is

$$\frac{\$25,000}{1,500 \text{ units}} = \frac{\$16.67}{\text{unit}}.$$

Tell students that when variable costs are added to fixed costs, we get *total costs*. Ask them to find the equation of the following lines and to explain how they got those equations:

- Total cost line
- Variable cost line, even though it is not shown on our graph

Correct responses are as follows:

- $y = \frac{50}{3}x + 50,000$. To get this equation, read the y-intercept from the graph and find another point, (1,500, 75,000), on the line by using the fact that the variable cost of 1,500 units is $25,000, so the total cost is $50,000 more. Finally, use the point-slope form to get the equation.
- $y = \frac{50}{3}x$ since the variable cost is $50,000 less than the total cost. So, the variable cost line is parallel to the total cost line, but its y-intercept is 0.

Tell students that revenue is the amount that you make from selling products and that, for our example, the revenue per unit is $100. Point out that the *revenue line* increases from zero upward and crosses the total cost line at the *break-even point*. That is the point at which the cost of producing products equals the revenue from selling those products. It is beyond this point that profits can finally be made. Ask students to find and explain the following:

- Equation of the revenue line
- Coordinates of the break-even point, interpreting them in the context of this problem

Correct responses are as follows:

- $y = 100x$ because the slope represents revenue per unit and the y-intercept is 0.
- (600, $60,000) because this is the solution to the system of equations: $y = 100x$ and $y = \frac{50}{3}x + 50,000$. The coordinates tell us that the cost of producing 600 units equals the revenue from selling those items, $60,000.

Finally, ask the students to find the revenue, total cost, and profit for selling 1,000 units of this product.
Correct responses are as follows:

- revenue $= \frac{\$100}{\text{unit}} \times 1,000$ units $= \$100,000$.
- total cost $= \frac{\$50/3}{\text{unit}} \times 1,000$ units $+ \$50,000 = \$66,666.67$.
- profit $=$ revenue $-$ total costs $= \$100,000 - \$66,666.67 = \$33,333$.

Projects

1. Construct a break-even graph from the following information: Fixed cost is $75,000, and the break-even point is where total cost is $95,000 and 10,000 units are sold.

2. Using the graph constructed in Question 1, calculate
   a. the loss if only 5,000 units are sold
   b. the profit if 20,000 units are sold

3. Do a break-even analysis for Widget World based on the data below:

Number of Widgets Sold	0	100	400	1,000
Revenue From Sales	0	$3,000	$12,000	$30,000
Total Cost	$500	$4,500	$16,000	$40,000

4. Have the students interview a local businessperson to determine how mathematics plays a role in their business.

Selected List of Formulas

PRESENT AND FUTURE VALUE

$$FV = PV(1+r)^n \text{ and } PV = \frac{FV}{(1+r)^n};$$

where

FV = future value
PV = present value
r = rate of interest (or investment)
n = number of years

Solving for r in our basic formula of $FV = PV(1+r)^n$, we obtain

$$r = \left(\frac{FV}{PV}\right)^{\frac{1}{n}} - 1 \text{ or } r = \sqrt[n]{\frac{FV}{PV}} - 1.$$

Solving for n in our basic formula of $FV = PV(1+r)^n$, we obtain

$$n = \log\frac{FV}{PV} \text{ divided by } \log(1+r)$$

(the natural log, ln, can also be used).

CONTINUOUS COMPOUNDING

$$FV = e^{rt},$$

where

e = the constant 2.718 . . .
r = the rate of interest or investment
t = the time or years of the investment

PRESENT AND FUTURE VALUE OF ANNUITIES

$$FV_{ordinary\ annuity} = Pmt\left[\frac{(1+r)^n - 1}{r}\right].$$

$$FV_{annuity\ due} = Pmt\left[\frac{(1+r)^n - 1}{r}\right] \times (1+r).$$

$$Pmt = FV_{annuity\ due} \times \frac{r}{[(1+r)^n - 1](1+r)}.$$

$$PV_{ordinary\ annuity} = Pmt\left[\frac{(1+r)^n - 1}{r}\right] \div (1+r)^n.$$

$$PV_{annuity\ due} = Pmt\frac{1 - \frac{1}{(1+r)^{n-1}}}{r} + 1.$$

STATISTICS

$$\text{Mean or } \bar{x} = \frac{\text{sum of the numbers}}{\text{number of data points}} = \frac{x_1 + x_2 + x_3 + \cdots + x_n}{n}.$$

$$\text{Standard deviation} = s = \sqrt{\sum\frac{(x_i - \bar{x})^2}{n - 1}}.$$

$$\text{Correlation coefficient} = r = \frac{n \sum (xy) - (\sum x)(\sum y)}{\sqrt{[n \sum x^2 - (\sum x)^2][n \sum y^2 - (\sum y)^2]}}.$$

$$\text{Standard deviation of a combined portfolio} = s_{portfolio} = \sqrt{\sum w_i w_j s_i s_j r_{ij}},$$

where

> w = the weight. Specifically, w_i is the weight of one of the investment and w_j = the weight of another investment.
>
> s = the standard deviation. Specifically, s_i is the standard deviation of one of the investments, and s_j is the weight of another investment.
>
> r_{ij} = the correlation between two investments.

Equation for a line:

$$y = mx + b,$$

where

$$m = \frac{\sum xy - \frac{(\sum x \sum y)}{n}}{\sum x^2 - \frac{(\sum x)^2}{n}}.$$

Excel
Spreadsheet Hints

Although spreadsheet technology can be quite complex, we concentrate on somewhat simple math tasks in this book. Furthermore, there are other spreadsheet programs. We used Excel in this book because it is a common one.

Within the book, we have given examples of spreadsheets, specifically in four chapters:

- Chapter 2, Teaching Example 2.2
- Chapter 3, Teaching Examples 3.1 and 3.2
- Chapter 4, Teaching Example 4.2
- Chapter 5, Teaching Example 5.2

One navigates around a spreadsheet with arrow and Pg keys and the mouse.

The basic math operations are as follows:

Addition	+
Subtraction	−
Multiplication	*
Division	/

Formulas and operations in Excel begin with an equals sign "=" (Lotus 1-2-3 uses the plus sign "+"). These can be simple arithmetic or logic statements, among many others, such as the following:

= C5 + C8 + D2	Add the values in cells C5, C8, and D2.
= SUM(E4:E10)	Sum the values in E4 through E10.
= IF(G8 > G2, H2, 0)	If the value in cell G8 is greater than the value that is in G2, then enter whatever value is in cell H2, but if G8 is not greater than G2, then enter a 0 (zero).

An absolute reference uses dollar signs "$" in the formula, such as $D$5, or a relative reference using just the cell address, such as D5. An absolute cell reference will reference only that specific cell, but a relative cell reference will change if it is moved or copied to another cell.

A fraction can be entered—for instance, 3¼ can be entered with a "=3" then a space and then "1/4." The resultant value will be shown as 3.25.

Many formulas are built into spreadsheets; for instance, the one for finding a mortgage payment (as illustrated in Chapter 5, Teaching Example 2) is

$$= \text{PMT (rate, nper, pv, fv, type),}$$

where

rate = interest rate per period
nper = number of periods
pv = the amount of the mortgage (present value)
fv = future value, which is left blank for a mortgage
type = "0" for a mortgage

These are only a few essentials for simple spreadsheet construction. You can use the "Help" menu in Excel for more information or consult the many spreadsheet books on this subject.

Money Glossary

Aggressive growth fund. A mutual fund seeking maximum capital gains and not current income.

Annuity due. An equal amount of money either received or required at the beginning of a period. This is in contrast to an ordinary annuity, which is a payment at the end of the period.

APR (annual percentage rate). The actual annual percent of the loan or interest produced by an investment. This allows for comparison between two like loans or investments that are quoted on a nonannual basis.

Balanced fund. A mutual fund seeking to preserve principal by investing in a mix of stocks and bonds.

Balance sheet. One of two basic business financial statements. It shows the assets and liabilities of a company. The other basic statement is the income statement. *See* Income statement.

Beta. How a stock or mutual fund fluctuates relative to the Dow Jones average or Standard & Poor's 500. For example, if a mutual fund has a beta of 1.10, then it will on average fluctuate 10% higher and lower than the standard, say, the Dow Jones average.

Bonds. A security issued by a corporation or the U.S. government that pays a regular interest payment. Usually the payment is made every 6 months.

Break-even point. The point in the finances of a business where it will be earning a profit. In other words, it is that point for a business that given its cost structure and volume of business, it will be making more money that its total costs.

Call feature. The right of a bond issuer to "call" or retire a bond before maturity, often as early as 5 years after it is issued.

Capital gains/losses. This is the investment gain (or loss), when one sells an investment, that is taxable.

Capitalization. This is the total worth of a company, given its price per share and how many shares are outstanding in the market. Major companies are called large-cap stocks, smaller companies are called small-cap stocks, and stocks that fall between them are called mid-cap stocks.

CD or certificate of deposit. An interest-bearing account usually offered by banks for a specific term. CDs can be for as short as 90 days and as long as 5 years.

Closed-end fund. A mutual fund that allows only a set number of shares. They are listed and traded on the major stock exchanges.

Commercial paper. Short-term notes issued by credit-worthy companies for usually less than 270 days (9 months).

Commodities. Investments of metals, oil, wheat, lumber, gold, or any other concrete items. This is in contrast to financial investments, which are "paper" investments.

Compound interest. Compound interest generates interest during the year, such as monthly or quarterly compounding. *See also* Simple interest.

Convertible bond. A bond that may be exchanged for common stock of the company.

Convertible preferred stock. Preferred stock that can be converted into common stock of the company.

Coupon. Refers to the interest payment of bonds, which is usually every 6 months.

CPI (consumer price index). This is the official amount of increases in prices over a period, usually monthly or yearly. It is measured by the Bureau of Labor Statistics.

Cyclical stocks. The stock of companies that tends to earn high income during a strong economy and low income during a downturn in the economy. Such companies are auto and building products.

Debenture. A bond that is unsecured by specific assets.

Debt ratio. A measure of a company's indebtedness, as measured by the ratio of the amount of debt divided by total assets.

Discount broker. A broker that gives no advice but simply buys and sells securities. The cost per transaction is considerably less than a full-service broker.

Dollar cost averaging. A method of investing in the stock market by regularly buying the same dollar amount of whatever shares one is interested in. When the stock or mutual fund is selling high, few shares will be purchased; when selling low, many more shares will be bought. Over time, then, you are buying more shares at a low price. This can be done with individual stocks or mutual funds.

Dow Jones Industrial Average. The average price of 30 selected stocks that is meant to be representative of our economy as a whole.

Earnings per share. The earnings of a company divided by the total numbers of shares outstanding.

Effective tax rate. This is the average tax rate that one is taxed at. This is in contrast to the marginal tax rate, which is the highest tax bracket one is taxed at.

Equities. Another name for common stocks.

Equity. A term that refers to what you own. Commonly, the word *equity* is meant as that portion of real estate you own outright over and above the outstanding mortgage.

Ex dividend. The first day after a stock trades without the immediate dividend.

FDIC or Federal Deposit Insurance Corporation. This is the government agency that insures bank deposits up to $100,000 per account.

Financial planner. A professional who helps people with financial calculations, investments, and problem solving. The most common designation is CFP (certified financial planner).

401(k). A popular investment at a company. Not all firms offer these accounts, but where they do, they are often the main investment for retirement. A similar-type plan is called a 403(b) plan at a nonprofit organization and a 457 plan at a municipality.

Fundamental analysis. Analysis of stocks by examining the health and management of a company or industry. This is in contrast to technical analysis, which analyzes just the movements and changes in prices.

Future dollars. The value calculated at some future time. This is versus "today's dollars."

Futures. A contract for the future delivery of a specified asset.

Future value. A value of money some time in the future, sometimes called future dollars. This is in contrast to present value, which is the value of money today.

GDP (gross domestic product). This is the total goods and services produced within a country.

GNMA or Ginnie Mae. Government-backed mortgage securities issued by the Government National Mortgage Association.

Growth and income fund. A mutual fund investing in established companies that have both an expectation of growth and steady dividend income.

Growth fund. A mutual fund investing in more established companies for growth and not for steady income.

Head-and-shoulders pattern. A pattern of stock prices resembling two "shoulders" on each side of a "head," or higher point.

Income. This is the general term used to indicate a company's revenues or sales. There is no hard-and-fast definition that a company must use. It can also indicate the company's net income or profit. Sometimes the term *margin* is used, as in *gross, operating,* or *net margin,* which means income, operating income, and net income.

Income statement. This is the general business statement that indicates the total income or revenue as well as the net income. *See* Income. The other basic statement is called the balance sheet, which lists the assets and liabilities of a company.

Index fund. A mutual fund that invests in a portfolio of stocks that duplicates an index, such as Standard & Poor's 500.

Investment banker. A firm that underwrites or sells new securities to the general public.

IRA or individual retirement account. A personal retirement account that can be added to each year a person is working.

Limit order. An order to buy or sell a stock at a specified price.

Load. A commission paid to invest in a mutual fund. Typically, this is 3% to 6% of the investment.

M-1. The total of all demand deposits, coins, and currency.

M-2. The value of M-1 plus savings accounts and money market funds.

M-3. The value of M-2 plus large deposits and institutional money market funds.

Margin. There are two meanings. First, it is the amount of money an investor must put down to buy a security on credit. It is then said that an investor buys something on "margin" and not full price. The second definition refers to an alternate meaning for income. *See* Income.

Marginal tax rate. This is the highest tax bracket one is taxed at. This is in contrast to the effective tax rate, which is the average tax rate that one is taxed at.

Money market account or fund. An account, or mutual fund, that invests in short-term interest instruments that pay interest based on current short-term interest rates. Mutual funds and banks offer these accounts.

Mortgage. A loan taken to purchase a house.

Mutual fund. An investment in which many stocks or other investments are combined together. Mutual funds can be a grouping of stocks, bonds, money market funds, or a combination of all of these. The prospectus will indicate what percentage of these will be the target of the fund. The grouping can be very specific, such as small-cap stocks, municipal bonds, or tax-free money market funds. Mutual funds are one of the most popular ways most people invest.

NAV. Net asset value, or the price of the mutual fund at any particular time. Total of the securities and other investments of a mutual fund divided by the number of shares invested. It is the value of one share of a mutual fund.

Net income. *See* Income.

Net present value (NPV). The value today of a series of future values. It is a "net" value because it nets the values together.

No-load. A mutual fund without a commission. They are contacted through an 800 telephone number, and transactions are conducted through the mail.

Because of some no-load mutual fund popularity, some charge a low-load of 2% to 3% to invest.

Odd lot. A number of shares less than 100, the usual number, which is called a round lot.

Open-end fund. The common form of mutual funds that do not have a set number of shares but allow whatever number of investors to invest in the fund.

Option. The right to buy or sell a stock, or futures contract, within a specified time.

Ordinary annuity. An amount of money received or required at the end of a period. This is in contrast to an annuity due, which is a payment at the beginning of a period.

P/E ratio. The ratio of the price of the stock divided by the earnings per share of the company. It is considered an important gauge of a company's performance because it measures how much each share of a company's stock is earning. The average P/E ratio of all companies in 2006 was about 18.

Private mortgage insurance (PMI). This is extra insurance that mortgage lenders often require when the mortgage amount is 80% or greater of the value of the house.

Preferred stock. Stock that is issued with a set amount of dividend to be paid each quarter. It changes in value mostly like a bond in that it changes in the opposite direction of interest rates.

Present-day dollars. A value, usually of dollars, expressed as the value right now. This is usually the result of a future value calculated in terms of the equivalent value today.

Present value. This is the value of money today, sometimes called present-day dollars. This is in contrast to future value, which is a value at some point in the future.

Prospectus. The official document of any security or mutual fund that identifies the details of the investment objective and assessment of the risks involved.

REIT. Real Estate Investment Trust, a closed-end mutual fund that invests in real estate and/or mortgages.

Repurchase agreement. Called "repos," they usually involve banks that hold government securities for a short-term agreement that will pay a current interest rate. It is intended that the borrower will "repurchase" the securities at the end of the agreement.

Risk. A measurement of variability or uncertainty, such as fluctuation of prices. It is usually expressed as a statistic of one standard deviation or the variability of an investment approximately 68% (two thirds) of the time.

Savings account. A general term for a savings fund but often refers to a bank account that is an interest-bearing account.

Sector fund. A mutual fund that invests in only a particular sector of the economy, such as only energy stocks, or in a particular region, such as only Asian companies.

Short sale. Selling a stock that one does not own by borrowing it temporarily from a brokerage firm.

Simple interest. Simple interest is the yearly interest without compounding. *See also* Compound interest.

Standard, & Poor's 500 or S&P 500. The average price of the 500 largest companies. This index is by capitalization, or the price of a stock times the number of traded shares. The largest 500 companies by this measure comprise the S&P 500 and is the standard by which investments in general are measured. This is in contrast to the Dow Jones Industrial Average, which is composed of only 30 stocks.

Stock. A security issued by a corporation. Common stock is one in which voting rights are given and is in general what is referred to as the stock of a company.

Supply and demand. The natural forces in the marketplace that indicate the price movements of a product or good, depending on how much supply or demand is present.

Tangibles. An investment that is real that you can actually touch, such as real estate or gold. This is opposed to intangible investments, such as stocks and bonds, which are only paper representations.

Technical analysis. The analysis of stocks by observing just the movements and changes in prices. This is in contrast to fundamental analysis, which analyzes the health and management of a company or industry.

Today's dollars. The same as present-day dollars. It is a value, usually of future dollars, that is expressed as the value right now.

Total return fund. A mutual fund that strives to achieve both growth and income by investing in growth stocks, high-dividend stocks, and bonds.

Treasury. A security issued by the U.S. government. Treasury bills (T-bills) are short-term securities with a maturity of 1 year or less. Treasury notes (T-notes) are usually for 2 to 10 years. Treasury bonds (T-bonds) are usually for 20 or 30 years.

Underwriting. The guaranteeing of the sale of new securities.

Unit trust. A bond mutual fund that buys bonds and holds them to maturity. There is no active management of the bond portfolio. The management fees are low, and the investor can anticipate a predictable return.

Warrant. A security offered by a company to buy stock at a specified price within a specified time.

Zero coupon bond. A nontraditional bond that pays no interest (although taxes are to be paid annually). It is generally assumed that the bond will not be called or cashed in by the company, so the bond will be in force to stated maturity.

Index

CORWIN PRESS

The Corwin Press logo—a raven striding across an open book—represents the union of courage and learning. Corwin Press is committed to improving education for all learners by publishing books and other professional development resources for those serving the field of PreK–12 education. By providing practical, hands-on materials, Corwin Press continues to carry out the promise of its motto: **"Helping Educators Do Their Work Better."**